WITH EMPTY HANDS

WITH EMPTY HANDS

The Message of
St Thérèse of Lisieux

Conrad de Meester, OCD

Translated from the French by Mary Seymour

BURNS & OATES
A Continuum imprint
LONDON • NEW YORK

First published in Great Britain in 2002 by
Burns & Oates (a Continuum imprint),
The Tower Building,
11 York Road,
London SE1 7NX
www.continuumbooks.com

And in the United States of America in 2002 by

ICS Publications,
2131 Lincoln Road, N.E.,
Washington, D.C. 20002, USA
www.icspublications.org

ISBN (UK) 0-860123-21-9
ISBN (USA) 0-935216-28-6

Acknowledgements

With Empty Hands is a translation and adaptation of *Les Mains vides* by Conrad de Meester, OCD, copyright © Editions du Cerf 1997, pour toute la francophonie.
Quotations from the works of St Thérèse of Lisieux are taken for the most part from the official translations © Washington Province of Discalced Carmelites, Inc. and are used with permission. On occasion, these translations have been adapted to suit the sense of the author's text.
Quotations from the Bible are taken for the most part from the Revised Standard Version copyright © 1973 by Division of Christian Education of the National Council of the Churches of Christ in the United States of America, used with permission.
Where it is necessary to approximate to St Thérèse's or the author's readings, RSV has been adapted and the Douay/Rheims and King James (AV) translations, as well as J. B. Phillips, *The New Testament in Modern English* copyright © J. B. Phillips 1960, have been drawn on.
Quotations from St John of the Cross are from *The Complete Works of St John of the Cross*, edited and translated by E. Allison Peers, copyright © Burns & Oates Limited 1935, 1953, used with permission.

Typeset by BookEns Ltd, Royston, Herts
Printed in Great Britain by MPG Books Ltd, Bodmin, Cornwall

Contents

Abbreviations

[MS] A   Manuscrit autobiographique dédié à Mère Agnès de Jésus (autobiographical manuscripts dedicated to Mother Agnes of Jesus)

[MS] B   Lettre à Soeur Marie du Sacré-Coeur, manuscrit autobiographique (Letter to Sister Marie of the Sacred Heart, autobiographical manuscript)

[MS] C   Manuscrit autobiographique dédié à Mère Marie de Gonzague (autobiographical manuscript dedicated to Mother Marie de Gonzague)

Au   Autobiography (*Histoire d'une âme: The Autobiography of St Thérèse of Lisieux*, third edition, tr. John Clarke, OCD, Washington, 1996 [contains A, B, C and other material])

CSG   Conseils et Souvenirs, Sister Geneviève [Céline Martin] (*A Memoir of My Sister*, tr. Carmelite Sisters of New York, New York, 1959)

DE   Derniers Entretiens (*St Thérèse of Lisieux, Her Last Conversations*, tr. John Clarke, OCD, Washington, 1977)

LC   Lettres des correspondants de Thérèse (Letters from Thérèse's correspondents, in *Letters of St Thérèse of Lisieux*, tr. John Clarke, OCD, Vol. I, 1877–1890, Vol. II, 1890–1897, Washington, 1982)

LT   Lettres de Thérèse (Letters from Thérèse, as LC). Joint LT/LC references are given as they appear at the top of the page in *Letters*. A single LT or LC reference is given when the other letter in the exchange is lost to us.

PA   Procès Apostolique, 1915–16 (Apostolic Process, 1915–16)

PN   Poésies de sainte Thérèse de l'Enfant Jésus (*The Poetry of St Thérèse of the Child Jesus*, tr. Donald Kinney, OCD, Washington, 1996)

PO   Procès de l'Ordinaire, 1910–11 (The Bishop's Process, 1910–11)

PR   Prières de St Thérèse de l'Enfant Jésus (*The Prayers of Saint Thérèse of Lisieux*, tr. Alethia Kane, OCD, Washington, 1997)

RP   Récréations pieuses de sainte Thérèse de l'Enfant Jésus (Pious Recreations of St Thérèse of the Child Jesus)

Introduction

WELL OVER A HUNDRED YEARS AGO, a fifteen-year-old girl named Thérèse Martin knocked at the door of the Carmel of Lisieux in Normandy. She was admitted and stayed there until she died nine years later. Why? you might ask. What was she supposed to do there? How could anyone as young as that persevere in the religious life in an Order like that at that time? Anyway, even if she did manage to do so, how would she turn out?

In fact, the adolescent Thérèse turned out very well indeed. Although she spent her life within the confines of four bare walls, so to speak, she was eventually declared a saint, universal patron of the missions, on a par with St Francis Xavier, and eventually a Doctor of the Church.

Admittedly, Thérèse did nothing spectacular. All she wanted was to live a hidden life with God, who was her Life. Yet her autobiography, written under obedience, became an instant bestseller after her death, and today she is loved and invoked by millions of Christians all over the world. She has had a vast and profound influence on theology, spirituality and the missionary apostolate, although a mere twenty-four years and 271 days elapsed between her birth in Alençon on 2 January 1873, and her death on 30 September 1897. It is almost as if she had been saintly from the cradle, or only needed the benefit of the sun's rays to warm the seeds of holiness in her soul.

In fact, nothing could be further from the truth. Like many other privileged souls, Thérèse had to grow and mature with much suffering and in total poverty. The brilliant intuitions of her faith are meaningful only when they are seen against the background of her personal life, with all its ups and downs and all its crises. Eventually she developed the capacity to represent everything in profoundly simple terms. This simplicity was the fruit of her ardent love, and of her imaginative, creative, but sorely tried attempt to reconcile the ultimately irreconcilable: in other words, to harmonize the total, unlimited response of God's lowly creature with God's infinite love. First of all, this daughter of a well-to-do clock-maker and an industrious lace-maker had to sense her *spiritual* poverty. It was some time before she learned to receive her love for God directly from God, and before she understood that the vigour of her actions stemmed from the power of his grace.

Thérèse's prophetic mission has had a tremendous impact on innumerable Christians since her autobiography was published in 1898. Pius XI, who canonized her in 1925, called her 'a Word of God'. Now her influence is more diffuse. It is mixed, as it were, like yeast in a dough. But Thérèse remains one of the foremost guides of contemporary spirituality. The way in which she talks about the sublime adventure of love to which every human being aspires is irresistible. She traces the warp and woof of the Christian way in everyday life and human relationships with instinctive tact and sensitive analogies; and she shows us how to use quite ordinary means to lead a profoundly Christian life in our immediate surroundings.

As the late Dom Helder Camara once observed:

> In the last analysis, sanctity is nothing but the Lord. He invites us to share in his holiness. But this shared holiness is neither an entitlement to glory nor a privilege reserved for exceptional souls, and much less a favor that we want to offer God. It is an obligation for all of us from the moment when, through baptism, we receive the sanctifying grace that makes us holy.

God wants to be our Liberator. Thérèse understood perfectly that the God of love (1 John 4: 7) is also the God of hope (Rom. 15: 13). She became aware of this more clearly after the failure of her first, 'do-it-yourself', ideal. Her experience was that of every Christian. Of course we all want to succeed in life, and many of us would like to love both Lord and neighbour sincerely and faithfully. Unfortunately we reach the limits of our capacities very quickly, and we seem to have the same experience with every ideal we pursue.

Thérèse teaches us not to remain in that helpless state, but to reach out to the Other, to Someone who is ready to help us. God wants to give himself entirely to his creatures. As the Good Shepherd, he is ready to look for his lost sheep on the mountain at the risk of his own life (Matt. 18: 12). Sooner or later, all of us who aspire to reach God will discover that we cannot 'take him over', as it were, but must humbly ask him to give himself to us.

Thérèse is the saint of hope. She shows us with what liberating force God can take possession of us and work through us. For he operated through her, starting from her immediate surroundings, and helped her to become a revolutionary of love.

Edith Stein, the Jewish philosopher and canonized saint, told a friend who had criticized Thérèse's literary style adversely:

> I am astonished by what you say about the Little Flower. Until now it had never entered my head to approach her in that way. My only impression when thinking about her was that I was faced by a human life uniquely and totally driven until the very end by the love of God. I know nothing greater than this, and it is a little of this which I would like as far as possible to carry over into my life and into the lives of those around me.

It is in a similar spirit that I should like to offer you my impressions of this unique adventure of Thérèse Martin with her God. A first version of this book appeared in 1972 as *Les Mains vides*. It reproduced the main points of my longer study, *Dynamique de la confiance (The Thrust of Assurance)*. The work was well received in the original Dutch and French editions, and in English (as *With Empty Hands*), Spanish, Japanese, Italian, Indonesian, Croatian, Korean and Swedish translations.

The intervening years saw the publication of the critical edition of *The Complete Works of Thérèse de Lisieux*, providing a wealth of new and vital information about the saint's life. Other publications on her life attracted wide interest. This book is an entirely new version of *With Empty Hands*, completely revised and rewritten, for I wanted to incorporate the latest findings on Thérèse. Furthermore, some of my opinions had matured in the meantime, and I wished to look more closely at Thérèse's psychology, the influence of her family environment, the development of her faith, her relationship with the various members of her family, her prayer life, and so on. I felt it was imperative to include the results of these studies in the new book.

I hope that if you are seeking the Lord you will find this little book a source of enlightenment for your own journey, and that you, like Thérèse, will come to know the joy of loving God and of being loved by God.

❧ 1 ❧

Love Beckons

THE FOURTEEN-YEAR-OLD THÉRÈSE MARTIN was a typical young girl. She was unusually intelligent, of course, but full of life. She enjoyed everything that was beautiful. All living things gave her pleasure. She liked to make friends, but she was also drawn to her freely chosen ideal. She was like a delicate rosebud, captivating and fragrant with promise.

Thérèse enjoyed many of the amenities of the middle-class life of that period. Her parents' business affairs had prospered and the family was well-to-do. She lived in comfort and was free to travel. If she had entered the social world of Lisieux, her home town, she would scarcely have been ignored or remained obscure. During the part of her adolescence she spent at home:

> [We] enjoyed together the most beautiful life young girls could dream about. Everything around us corresponded with our tastes; we were given the greatest liberty; I would say our life on earth was the *ideal of happiness.* (A 49 v; Au 106)

The Dawn

Thérèse had an equable temperament, although this had not always been the case. She was scarcely four and a half years old when her mother died of cancer, at a very critical time in the little girl's psychological and emotional development. Mother and child had enjoyed a happy, loving relationship. When death severed the bond, Thérèse lost the tender warmth that a child of that age needs and craves. No one could compensate for that loss. As a result, Thérèse became shy, vulnerable and hypersensitive, especially with outsiders. She felt secure only in the sheltered nest of her home, 'Les Buissonnets'. Even there, in spite of her family's love and attention, Thérèse could not help indulging in frequent pitiful outbursts of tears. 'I was really unbearable because of my extreme touchiness,' she wrote self-deprecatingly when she recalled those days. She was so sensitive that when 'I began to cheer up, I'd begin to cry again for having cried' (A 44 v).

Thérèse became acutely withdrawn at this time. She found it distressing to be aware of so many varied possibilities yet to be unable to take advantage of them because of her extreme shyness and reticence. Nevertheless, her persistent, even if ineffective, efforts to change her character made her unusually determined. She forged a will of her own. Later in life, Thérèse was never easily dissuaded from a course of action once she had decided on it.

In the meantime, a momentous change occurred on Christmas Day 1886. The family had just come back from Midnight Mass. Monsieur Martin was tired and perhaps a little grumpy. With some annoyance (a rare event for someone so kind and considerate), he observed that, although she was now thirteen, Thérèse still enjoyed putting her slippers by the fireplace as French children did at the time. 'For the last time, thank goodness!' he added, rather testily.

She had never heard her beloved father say anything like that before. He was always so gentle and caring. Suddenly the mirror where she saw herself reflected had cracked. Now his features seemed distorted. Papa was no longer a kindly reflection but a force to reckon with.

She understood more painfully and clearly than ever before that it was time to abandon 'the swaddling clothes of a child'. She had often tried to do so in the past, but now she had to succeed in throwing off childish things. Although, as usual, tears were already welling in her eyes, for once in her life she kept them back. She mastered a very difficult situation, went through the experience of 'growing up in an instant', and became 'strong and courageous' on the spot.

Thérèse attributed this minor psychological victory to Jesus, the Child in the manger whom she had just received in the Eucharist:

On that luminous night which sheds such light on the delights of the Holy Trinity, Jesus, the gentle, little Child of only one hour, changed the night of my soul into rays of light ... Since that night I have never been defeated in any combat, but rather walked from victory to victory. (A 44 v; Au 97)

God's own strength had invaded her very psyche. All the vain efforts of previous years were now gathered together in a permanent state of strength. Later, Thérèse referred to this incident of Christmas 1886 as 'the grace of my complete conversion'. She no longer suffered from an almost neurotic form of self-obsession. She was no longer in that 'very narrow circle in which I was turning without knowing how to come out' (A 46 v). Thérèse soon made up for lost time, and 'the third period of my life, the most beautiful and the most filled with graces from heaven' (A 45 v) began.

Now the doors of life seemed to open before her young eyes and reveal a world waiting to be explored. Cured of her hypersensitivity, Thérèse enthusiastically embraced all the sources of enrichment available to a young girl of her age and background: study, travel and friendships.

But what was happening in the heart of this teenager who was actually so much more mature than her peers? Something a little less than extraordinary, in fact, and even quite contrary to the first reactions of a normal girl to the adventures of life as they unfold. A young person is usually captivated by everything or by nothing. But in Thérèse's case most things were already quite relative. Her innermost being would soon be fully open in a special way. For her, everything would revolve about a fixed point endowed with an absolute value. From now on, her life would be centered on the unique, enduring love that had conquered her heart. Her precociously mature love was different from that of other young people, for she had already chosen the one point on which it would be focused. Nevertheless, she was no different from the other people of her age in wanting to abandon herself totally to her longing, her dream ideal.

The ideal that had captivated the youngest Martin sister was neither an ideology nor an object, but a human being unlike any other. It was Jesus himself. Thérèse aspired to love Jesus passionately, with all her heart. Life was a gift *from* him and must be spent *for* him. She knew that she had been summoned by creative love, and wanted to respond to the challenge of that unique love by assenting to it wholly and completely, with all her being.

It is important to understand that Thérèse did not think of Jesus as a distant historical personage who had lived in nebulously remote times. He was very present and close to her. Most important of all, he really loved her. Later in life she scarcely mentioned the resurrection as such in her writings. For Thérèse it was self-evident that Jesus was alive now and present now. After all, you don't need to talk about the air you breathe day in day out, in every natural second. Jesus was the divine and holy atmosphere in and through which she lived. She found signs of him everywhere. For her the earth was limpid and clear, for it was Jesus' world, the universe of her Beloved.

On one occasion when she described this springtime of her life, Thérèse quoted the works of the sixteenth-century Spanish mystic, St John of the Cross. Two poems, *The Dark Night* and *The Spiritual Canticle*, stress the power of love and its shaping of a human being's spiritual journey:

> On that glad night,
> in secret, for no one saw me,
> with no other light or guide
> than the one that burned in my heart.
> This guided me
> more surely than the light of noon
> to where he was awaiting me
> – him I knew so well –
> there in a place where no one appeared.
> (*Dark Night*, stanzas 3 and 4; A 49 r)

> Following your footprints
> maidens run lightly along the way;
> the touch of a spark,
> the special wine,
> cause flowings in them from the balsam of God.
> (*Spiritual Canticle*, stanza 25; A 48 r)

She also cited the Song of Solomon: 'When I should find thee without, I would kiss thee; yea, I should not be despised' (Song of Solomon, 8: 1; A 48 r).

Thérèse realized that God himself was teaching her to love and suffusing her with his own love:

> The way I was walking was so straight, so clear, I needed no other guide but Jesus. ... [Jesus] willed to have his mercy shine out in me. Because I was little and weak he lowered himself to me, and he instructed me secretly in the *things* of his *love*. (A 48 v; Au 105)

In this light, even the Old Testament became a new, vital and personal experience. Before long she applied Ezekiel's words to herself:

> Passing by me, Jesus saw that the time had come for me to be *loved*, he entered into a covenant with me and I became *his own*. He spread his mantle over me. (A 47 r; Au 101)

Although Thérèse was still free to choose her future life, she was no longer free. She saw that from now on her life would unfold under the sign of Jesus, and that this would determine everything else.

As I have suggested, Thérèse's spiritual evolution cannot be compared with the usual process among people of her age. She was destined to become a model for countless other souls. She began to live her Christian life with intensity at a very early age. She was barely nine years old when she chose sanctity as her ideal. Shortly after that, she realized that she would have to go through an immense amount of suffering before reaching her goal. She accepted this. True to her nature, she chose everything, for she 'did not want to be a saint by halves' (A 10 v).

At the time of her first Communion she described her meeting with the Lord as '... a fusion; they were no longer two. Thérèse had vanished as a drop of water is lost in the immensity of the ocean. Jesus alone remained; he was the Master, the King' (A 35 r).

The graces that flowed to her from the Eucharist were so powerful that her willingness to suffer grew more intense. She did not need to hunt out occasions of suffering, for they were already a reality in her life. For example, at a retreat the chaplain gave for children preparing for first Communion, Thérèse took to heart his admonitions on death, hell, sacrilegious Communions and the Last Judgement. The superior of the convent died in the midst of these stern warnings, and the *abbé* had to stop his course of instruction. As a result, however, Thérèse's delicate conscience had suffered the unfortunate effects of a stern catechesis for the first time. Nevertheless, she was able to receive her first Communion in perfect bliss. The following year, however, what turned out to be her doubts and scruples came back to haunt her for eighteen long months, until, after asking her four siblings in heaven to intercede for her and thus free her from this persecution, she was flooded with an inward peace that never left her.

Then, of course, there were the difficulties with her sensitive nature, and, at Christmas 1886, the harsh effects of her feeling of helplessness, alleviated then by her conviction of God's liberating mercy. The lack of proportion between her efforts and the unexpected results prompted her to write:

> The work I had been unable to do in ten years was done by Jesus in one instant, contenting himself with my good will which was never lacking. (A 45 v; Au 98)

> I had to buy, so to speak, this inestimable grace through my desires. (A 43 v; Au 91)

Now that she had finally lost her touchiness and her doubts, Thérèse was psychologically capable of paying due attention to her neighbour. She summarized her discovery thus: 'I felt charity enter into my soul, and the need to forget myself and to please others; since then I've been happy' (A 45 v).

Six months later she happened on a book by the Abbé Arminjon, which her father had borrowed from the Carmelites. It was quite fascinating, and she read it from cover to cover:

This reading was one of the greatest graces in my life. I read it by the window of my study, and the impressions I received are too deep to express in human words. All the great truths of religion, the mysteries of eternity, plunged my soul into a state of joy not of this earth. I experienced already what God reserves for those who love him (not with the eye but with the heart), and seeing the eternal rewards had no proportion to life's small sacrifices, I wanted to love, to love Jesus with a passion, giving him a thousand proofs of my love while it was possible. (A 47 v; Au 102)

At this time Thérèse found it a veritable blessing to talk freely about all these things to Céline, her sister and senior by four years. Sharing her impressions brought new insights and aroused an even more profound and heartfelt enthusiasm in her. Céline was more than a sister, for Thérèse called her 'my other self'. When she was with Céline, Thérèse was as entirely herself as she would be later in prayer:

Céline had become the confidante of my thoughts. ... Jesus formed bonds in our hearts stronger than blood. ... The sparks of love he sowed so generously in our souls, and the delicious and strong wine he gave us to drink made all passing things disappear before our eyes, and from our lips came aspirations of love inspired only by him. How sweet were the conversations we held each evening in the belvedere. ... It appears we were receiving graces like those granted to the great saints ... how light and transparent the veil was that hid Jesus from our gaze! Doubt was impossible, faith and hope were unnecessary, and Love made us find on earth the One whom we were seeking. 'When I should find thee without, I would kiss thee; yea, I should not be despised' [Song of Solomon]. (A 47 v–48 r; Au 103–4)

The Call

When the instincts of a wife and mother began to awaken in Thérèse, she knew that she would keep their fulfillment for Jesus alone. One Sunday after Mass she suddenly noticed an image of Jesus on the Cross. She was deeply moved by the blood flowing from the hand of her crucified Lord, and her heart was overwhelmed by a powerful desire to share his work of saving souls. From then on she seemed constantly to hear the cry, 'I thirst!'

> After this unique grace, my desire to save souls grew each day, and I
> seemed to hear Jesus say to me what he said to the Samaritan woman:
> 'Give me to drink!' It was a true interchange of love: to souls I was
> giving the blood of Jesus, to Jesus I was offering these same souls
> refreshed by the divine dew. I slaked his thirst and the more I gave him
> to drink, the more the thirst of my poor little soul increased, and it was
> this ardent thirst he was giving me as the most delightful drink of his
> love. (A 46 v; Au 100–1)

Now that she had occasion to meet people beyond the family circle, the contemplative dimension of her life took shape, even in the way in which she thought of people and humanity as a whole. Everything in her aimed at one ultimate goal: Jesus. She loved him in everyone, and she loved everyone in him. She wanted to give him to everyone and to help everyone come closer to God. She saw this as her special vocation at this time. Not surprisingly, she was particularly keen on the missionary apostolate. Nevertheless, the future patron of missions decided that it would be more beneficial to live her missionary vocation in prayer as a Carmelite. She was sure that she could devote herself more appropriately to the advantage of the Church 'in the monotony of an austere life' (CSG 109), and 'without ever seeing the fruit of her labors' (CSG 152).

This was neither an escape from the world nor a betrayal of humankind. On the contrary, Thérèse wanted to bring the entire world with her to the Carmel of Lisieux as if to a workshop where she could labor for the very soul of humanity. She looked at the world by associating herself with Jesus' love and therefore with an approximation to his own loving gaze. In one and the same impulse, she wanted to pray that God's name should be truly hallowed and that his kingdom would be established among human beings. This was how she planned to work for the salvation of souls.

By the time she entered Carmel, her ambition would seem to have assumed a social dimension: 'I came to save souls and especially to pray for priests' (A 69 v).

That Thérèse should say 'souls' for humanity or people was typical of her and should not be taken negatively. She wanted to meet all humankind in the most profound sense possible, and was well aware of the part she might play and the degree of responsibility she might assume in the divine transformation of the human condition:

> It is because Jesus has so incomprehensible a love for us that he wills to do nothing without us. The Creator of the universe awaits the prayer of a poor little soul to save other souls redeemed like it at the price of all his blood. (LT 135)

Towards the end of her life she developed a highly generous, all-encompassing apostolic awareness with a primary emphasis on the neighbors whom she saw every day – her community. She was very attentive to the members of her Carmel. Of course this aspect of her spirituality has especially endeared her to all Christians, both lay people and religious. All sorts and conditions of people are not only attracted to her but find they can relate to her easily. This little saint who, once she took up the religious life, never set foot outside the cloister, teaches us that we can all be apostles and missionaries in our God-given vocation, wherever we find ourselves. Simply by our charity, prayer and the crosses of our everyday lives, and in the petty tasks and sacrifices of the daily grind, we can all spread God's kingdom. Thérèse's apostolic impulse was immensely far-reaching and universally ambitious:

> O Jesus ... I would like to travel over the whole earth ... one mission alone would not be sufficient for me, I would want to preach the Gospel on all the five continents simultaneously and even to the most remote isles. (B 3 r; Au 192–3)

Later on she would discover how this soaring ambition could be fulfilled in *love*, the motor power of the Mystical Body of Christ: 'In the heart of the Church, my Mother, I shall be *Love*. Thus I shall be everything, and thus my dream will be realized' (B 3 v).

It is possible to love anywhere and at any time. From Thérèse of Lisieux to Mother Teresa of Calcutta the differences are only external. In God's eyes nothing has more value than the love that can permeate a human life: 'Though I speak with the tongues of men and of angels, and have not love, I am become as sounding brass, or a tinkling cymbal' (1 Cor. 13: 1).

Before she reached the age of fifteen, Thérèse Martin had decided to live for God as soon as possible and as radically as she might be able. Her desire, indeed 'the certitude of a divine call' (A 26 r), immunized her, so to speak, against all family objections to her entering a religious order when she was so young, and against all judicious advice. She was sure that it was now time to act:

> [He was awaiting me in Carmel.] Before 'resting in the shadow of him whom I desired', I was to pass through many trials, but the divine call was so strong that had I been forced to pass through flames, I would have done it out of love of Jesus. (A 49 r; Au 106)

She surmounted every obstacle: whether posed by her father, her spiritual director, the bishop, or Carmel itself. During her trip to Rome she even pleaded her vocation with the pope.

At long last, on 9 April 1888, with love as her ideal – and almost her only baggage – she found herself before the door of the cloister. For the last time she embraced her beloved 'papa' and other members of her family. Still with some apprehension, she crossed the threshold of the Order in Lisieux and never returned.

Was Thérèse ready to take such a step? In fact, this fifteen-year-old adolescent had the mature attitude of a young woman of twenty. A great light shone with clarity in the depths of her soul and the joy of loving Jesus carried her forward: 'I am his and he is mine!' This was the constant theme of her assurance. Thérèse compared her youthful enthusiasm to the delicious wine 'that rejoices the heart and makes one forget so many things'. Together with the apostle Paul, she was convinced that nothing could separate her from God, to whom she was surely joined. She was living in 'the Heaven of Love' (A 52 v).

Thérèse was aware of what she was doing:

This happiness was not passing. It didn't take its flight with 'the illusions of the first days'. *Illusions*, God gave me the grace not to have A SINGLE ONE when entering Carmel. I found the religious life to be *exactly* as I had imagined it, no sacrifice astonished me. (A 69 v; Au 149)

The realism of such remarks shows that she was sufficiently mature to take that decisive step. Of course there was still work to be done before she was an accomplished entrant to the Order, but there was time to learn and develop. Admittedly, her exceptional foresight could not accurately predict or ward off the painful changes that would result from future suffering. But learning to cope with such experiences is part of personal growth.

Perhaps the example of her sister Pauline (Sr Agnes of Jesus) helped Thérèse to be so determined. So often in God's plan we are a gift to one another. After the death of their mother, Pauline had become a 'second mama' (A 13 r) for little Thérèse, and her ideal (A 6 r). Pauline's departure for Carmel (followed a few years later by that of a second sister, Marie) was a psychological factor that indirectly sealed Thérèse's assurance of her vocation and God's grace. Nevertheless, in the last analysis, Thérèse knew very well that ultimately her difficult decision was guided only by a free acceptance of a plan she perceived as coming from, and desired by, God himself. That was how she expressed it some years later, when she looked back on her life with a judgement already refined and enlightened by her intimacy with God: 'It was surely only love of Jesus that could help me surmount these difficulties and the ones that followed' (A 53 v).

The Desert

What did Carmel mean to Thérèse? In her childhood she had dreamed of living a solitary life in a remote desert with her sister Pauline. Later, when she was offered an explanation of a Carmelite vocation, she responded with the feeling that 'Carmel was the *desert* where God wanted her to go and hide'. And so it was there she wanted to go 'for Jesus alone' (A 26 r), for an adventure with God, unnoticed, in a spot where he alone could be found. When she actually entered the Order, she knew immediately that she had not made a mistake:

> My desires were at last accomplished; my soul experienced a PEACE so sweet, so deep, it would be impossible to express it. For seven years and a half that inner peace has remained my lot, and has not abandoned me in the midst of the greatest trials. . . . Everything thrilled me . . . I felt as though I had been transported into a desert. Our little cell, above all, filled me with joy. But the joy I was experiencing was *calm*, the lightest breeze did not undulate the quiet waters. . . . I was fully recompensed for all my trials. With what deep joy I repeated those words: 'I am here forever and ever.' (A 69 v; Au 148)

Thérèse reached out as intensely as she could for the state of being that Paul had proposed to the Colossians: 'Set your affection on things above, not on things on the earth. For you are dead and your life is hid with Christ in God' (1 Col. 3: 2–3).

We must not forget that a vocation is a grace from God. The uninitiated might think it would be more understandable if we had two lives to dispose of: one to be tested and the other to be kept in reserve. If the first one failed, then the second one would supply an alternative. But Thérèse, like the rest of us, had only one life, and she pledged it all to Jesus only in order to live it in the desert without any expectation of another chance to relive it in a different context.

When she considered her memorable trip to Rome across Switzerland and Italy in 1887, Thérèse wrote:

> Never had I been surrounded with so much luxury . . . joy isn't found in the material objects surrounding us but in the inner recesses of the soul. One can possess joy in a prison cell as well as in a palace. The proof of this: I am happier in Carmel even in the midst of interior and exterior trials than in the world surrounded by the comforts of life, and even the sweetness of the paternal hearth! (A 65 r; Au 137)

Thérèse freely chose to leave everything behind her. Eventually she would experience the actual crossing of the desert. For the present, she must contemplate the solitude and silence of her new home with its bare walls and sober furnishings. This new life, with its daily hours of prayer, restricted hours of sleep, frugal diet and the winter cold, seemed austere and monotonous. But that realization was not to be her most purifying experience, as we shall see. Indeed, she found that her new way of life brought her a certain liberation, for now she could say goodbye to the sheltered bourgeois life of her father's house and follow her own spiritual inclination.

Did she know what the new life might have in store for her? No. The future is seldom clear to any of us. We know where it begins but not where it will end. History records other crossings of the desert, such as that of Moses and his people. Yet they longed to return to the land of familiar haunts and material security, and their hearts had hardened and rebelled. The desert is the very antithesis of the sheltered nest. It was a very bold decision for Thérèse to agree to make the desert her life, to commit herself to God unconditionally, to concern herself with his love alone, and to welcome everything within that perspective.

We can say without exaggeration that few young girls have loved as passionately as Thérèse loved her Lord Jesus. In order to find her Beloved, she walked through the very heart of the desert, for, after all, that was the quickest way to find him. Her spiritual father, St John of the Cross, had taught her 'to go to the *All* by way of the *Nothing*'. Solitude did not mean Void. It implied a pleasurable walk to the dwelling-place of her Beloved in the oasis. This gave privation a meaning and the desert a new dimension of *profundity*.

But when she crossed that spiritual desert, the Beloved was not only in the oasis. He also accompanied her on the journey. He was an elusive companion perhaps, but he was always close at hand, and visible to a prayerful soul's eyes of faith and joy.

While Céline was away on holiday, Thérèse had written to her:

> Céline, the vast solitudes, the enchanting horizons opening up before you must be speaking volumes to your soul. I myself see nothing of all that, but I say with Saint John of the Cross: 'My Beloved is the mountains, and lonely, wooded valleys, etc.' And this Beloved instructs my soul. He speaks to it in silence, in darkness. (LT 135; LC 148)

At times, however, Thérèse felt that night was falling on her desert. It seemed as if everything might vanish, and darkness descend on her. Then she no longer perceived the Invincible, and she suffered then more than at any other time in her life to date. Now she knew that the heart of the desert was the desert of the heart. She no longer felt the hand that was leading her. Trembling, she looked about her. If we had had this experience, we would have been tempted to think: He is nowhere, there is nothing but emptiness!

But Thérèse did not reason in that way. Hers was the logic of the Gospel: 'Blessed are they that have not seen, and yet have believed' (John 20: 29). Move on then! Forge ahead! Don't retrace your steps! – she might have said. To quote the French writer and intrepid aviator, Saint-Exupéry: 'Once the route has been mapped out, you have to follow it.' The more risky Thérèse's venture appeared, the more certain she was that the track would not end in a mirage. She consulted her compass, the Bible. She read the desert writings of St John of the Cross avidly, and found the encouragement to carry on searching for her goal till the very end.

Thérèse began her hazardous journey in the company of some twenty women of all ages. These women made up a small caravan (to pursue the metaphor). They were a column of the people of God, a contingent in the Church of Christ that was small but well to the forefront of its pilgrimage. Thérèse owed them a great deal, for they were her Carmelite sisters who shared their personal experiences with her and passed on the lore that would help her to continue into the future. They came from different backgrounds and were a quite varied group in spite of the brown habit they all wore. But a common purpose had brought them to Carmel, and they were all inspired by the same Spirit of God.

The personal qualities of the members of Thérèse's community were possibly less impressive than those in an average Carmelite house. There were a few strong personalities among them, but, in general, they were ordinary women with shortcomings as well as virtues. A few even bore the marks of deep psychological conflicts. Thérèse became aware of these aspects of her community only little by little:

> ... a lack of judgment, of good manners, touchiness in certain characters; all these things which don't make life very agreeable. I know very well that these mortal infirmities are chronic, that there is no hope of a cure. ... (C 28 r; Au 246)

Whenever possible, she chose the side of the most disadvantaged:

> This is the conclusion I draw from this: I must seek out in recreation, on free days, the company of Sisters who are the least agreeable to me in order to carry out with regard to these wounded souls the office of the Good Samaritan. A word, an amiable smile, often suffice to make a sad soul bloom. (C 28 r; Au 246)

Thérèse committed herself to these Sisters with unlimited devotion. This showed the healthiness of her spiritual ambitions. To love God is to love, to an ever-increasing extent and in a tangible way, all those who surround us. *They* are our neighbors: 'For the poor you always have with you', as Jesus said (John 12: 8).

Many people, like Thérèse, find that they are in a spiritual desert. A desert can settle in your heart almost imperceptibly, whether in the clamor of a big city, in your everyday work, or in your social relations. It can take on a hopeless appearance because of ill health or a psychological handicap, of loneliness in marriage or a lack of understanding between friends, and of course old age, grief, boredom, and even financial insecurity. Surely we have all experienced the desert in one way or another?

But Thérèse tells us that the desert experience is the time for greater trust. But don't try to go it alone! Jesus is there with you, she says. Convert your difficulties into love. Thérèse's personal desert became the 'heart of the Church'. The heart of the Church is wherever we choose to pray or work or love or suffer, but with our gaze fixed on our crucified Lord.

Through the eyes of Christ, Thérèse discovered all humanity. She became and remains 'of the Church', universal, responsible for 'thousands of souls' (LT 135). As for suffering, she deliberately adopted it as her life's goal, and aimed to be an apostle 'through prayer and sacrifice!' (A 50 r). When Céline in her turn thought she might be called to Carmel, Thérèse encouraged her with an unexpected argument: 'Fear nothing. Here you will find more than anywhere else the cross and *martyrdom*!' (LT 167).

Love never disappeared from her horizon. Thérèse referred to it constantly in her letters on her desert theme:

> I want to give all to Jesus, and I don't want to give to the creature even one *atom* of my love. (LT 76)

> My only desire is to do the will of Jesus always. (LT 74)

> There is only Jesus who *is*; all the rest is *not*. ... Let us love him, then, unto folly; let us save souls for him ... our mission is to forget ourselves and to reduce ourselves to nothing. ... We are so insignificant ... and yet Jesus wills that the salvation of souls depends on the sacrifices of our love. ... Ah, let us understand his look! ... There is only one thing to do during the night, the one night of life which will come only once, and this is to love, to love Jesus with all the strength of our heart and to save souls for him so that he may be loved! ... Oh, make Jesus loved! (LT 96)

Although she was closely united to her religious 'caravan' through support and encouragement, Thérèse experienced certain attempts to restrain her. The behaviour of some Sisters was tantamount to trying to persuade the others to temper the ardency of their pursuit of holiness – or even to take a 'breather' – thus tacitly declaring that the 'expedition' was impossible and should be discontinued. One confessor even reproached Thérèse for her desires 'to become a saint and to love God as much as St Teresa of Avila had loved him'. He thought that her aspirations smacked of presumption. Thérèse's reaction was typical: 'But, Father, how can these desires be over-ambitious since our Lord said, "Be perfect even as your heavenly Father is perfect"?' (PA 605).

In a letter to Céline she insisted:

... to be perfect as your Heavenly Father is perfect! Ah! Céline, our infinite desires are not, then, either dreams or fantasies, since Jesus himself has given us this commandment! (LT 107)

She often spoke of the 'folly' of love and of its mad aspirations as the only adequate response to God's own insane love for mankind.

The Sand

You can see only sand and sky in the desert. For a long time Thérèse was attracted by the sky, for she had always had a presentiment that she would die young and be 'up there' very soon.

Now she discovered the symbolism of sand. A grain of sand had no identity; it was so tiny it was almost invisible. She saw it as representing the hidden life, self-effacement and poverty – all objectives she was pursuing so intensely. The grain of sand was wonderfully appropriate to the realm of her imagination during the early years of her religious life. After all, she was living in a religious house, hidden from the eyes of the world. And then she certainly preferred those small gestures of love that escaped notice and by now had become second nature to her. At the same time, her prayer had dried up entirely and she felt almost crushed by suffering. This period of her spiritual life might be described as governed by a desire to disappear completely in order to become a source of love for Jesus that would be even more pure than before. It was impossible, so she reasoned, to be full of self and full of God at one and the same time.

Thérèse probably received the image of a grain of sand from her sister Pauline (Sr Agnes) just before she became a religious herself. She identified with it immediately:

Ask that your little daughter always remain a little grain of sand, truly unknown, truly hidden from all eyes, that Jesus alone may be able to see it; and that it may become smaller and smaller, that it may be reduced to *nothing*. (LT 49)

It was not a question of *being* small but of *becoming* smaller and smaller. 'He must grow and I must decrease.' These words of the Baptist summarized all her efforts. Her aspirations to littleness became more and more exacting and all-encompassing. She regretted she was not yet 'small enough, or light enough' (LT 54).

On the day of her profession she prayed:

> Jesus, be *everything*! ... May the things of earth never be able to trouble my soul, and may nothing disturb my peace. Jesus, I ask you for nothing but peace, and also love, infinite love without any limits other than yourself; love that is no longer I but you, my Jesus. Never let me be a burden to the community, let nobody be occupied with me, let me be looked on as one to be trampled underfoot [so that] I may be looked upon and forgotten like your little grain of sand, Jesus. (PR 38)

Later on, Pauline would sum up the salient features of Thérèse's first five years in the monastery as 'humility and the utmost care to be faithful, even in the smallest things' (PO 444).

The perfection of love always remained Thérèse's *ideal*, but she also believed, candidly during these early years, that love would also be the sole *pathway* towards her ideal. Admittedly, she still had much to learn with regard to her helplessness. For the time being, her desire for humility and self-effacement coincided entirely with love – a magnificent perspective and synthesis! She longed to become ever more lowly in order to love all the more – indeed, in order to love more ardently, more purely, more constantly, and to begin again and again. Like others before her, Thérèse experienced her weakness, but she tried to transform it to accord with these three aspects of love. Her weakness became an accomplice of her love:

> Jesus, on the road to Calvary, fell three times, and, you, poor little child, you would not be like your *Spouse* if you would not be willing to fall a hundred times if necessary to prove your love for him, rising with greater strength than before your fall! (LT 81)

> Oh, how it costs to give Jesus what he asks! What *joy* that it costs. ...

What an unspeakable joy to carry our crosses FEEBLY. .... Oh, let us
not lose the trial that Jesus is sending us, it is a gold mine to be
exploited. Are we going to miss the chance? ... The grain of sand
wants to get to work, without *joy*, without *courage*, without *strength*, and
it is all these titles that will facilitate the enterprise for it; it wants to
work through love. The *martyrdom is beginning*. (LT 82)

This desire to suffer and to forget herself was not symptomatic
of any masochism or dolorism in the young Carmelite. Her
writings clearly attest to the fact that her courage in suffering
was born of her love for the person of Jesus himself in order to
please *him alone* by sharing his lot as fully as possible, but
without neglecting the least of her duties or responsibilities as a
Carmelite:

Pray for the poor little grain of sand, that the grain of sand be always in
its place, that is to say, under the feet of all, that no one may think of it,
that its existence be, so to speak, *unknown*. The grain of sand does not
desire to be *humbled* – this is still too glorious since one would be
obliged to be occupied with it. It desires only one thing, to be
FORGOTTEN, counted for *nothing*! But it desires to be seen by Jesus.
(LT 95)

The glory of Jesus, that is all; as for my own glory, I abandon it to him,
and, if he seems to forget me, well then, He is free ... since I am no
longer my own but his! ... And he will more quickly grow tired of
making me wait than I shall grow tired of waiting for him! (LT 103)

Thérèse often used the expression 'to be little' at this time
and continued to do so later in life. However, it underwent a
remarkable shift as time went on. In her first years as a
Carmelite, 'littleness' was especially synonymous with *humility*
in the service of her love for God. Later, to be little or to be
child-like was to bear a meaning well beyond humility, which
must obviously remain as a fundamental attitude to God and a
requirement of pure love. For Thérèse littleness would come to
be essentially synonymous with *confident hope*, a child's
confidence with regard to its father. She would no longer
think of littleness in terms of her pursuit of God's love but

much more in terms of God's merciful love *for her*, a love she received and accepted quite simply.

In this first phase, of course, Thérèse was guided by the virtue of hope. She ardently hoped to reach the summit of love by the power of God's grace, and to do so quickly, very quickly. But she needed to be much more deeply convinced of her own powerlessness before centering her hope solely on God's merciful and provident fidelity towards her. Indeed, before Thérèse could reach the existential awareness that it is God himself and God alone who sanctifies us, she had to live through a long night of futile striving (see John 21). But to live is to grow, and many people struggle with God before yielding to him.

From the beginning of her novitiate, Thérèse wanted to achieve sanctity by her own power, that is, through the strength of her love for Jesus. Her thinking was too much 'I'll give everything to Jesus', and too little 'Jesus will give me everything'. This attitude is best illustrated by the passage below from a letter dated 10 July 1890. Thérèse had been cloistered for a little over two years, but the 'sacred fire' was still roaring, and nothing had shaken her conviction that she would become a saint provided her love continued to grow. Of course she knew that she was weak, but she still considered her weakness as an almost exceptional occasion for her to love more purely. Later, full of confidence, she was to surrender her weakness to the Lord as an opportunity for him to share his merciful love with her more fully.

She wrote to her cousin, Marie Guérin:

> If you are nothing, you must not forget that Jesus is *All*, so you must lose your little nothingness in His *infinite* All and think only of this uniquely lovable *All*. ... When we see ourselves as so miserable, then we no longer wish to consider ourselves, and we look only on the unique Beloved! ... Dear little Marie, I know no other means of reaching perfection but [love]. Love, how well our heart is made for that! (LT 109)

At this time she saw love as the only road to perfection. But before she discovered what she was to call her 'little way'

Thérèse had to undergo many changes in the process of spiritual growth. It would take six years, after a blinding intuition of God's saving mercy, before she could write: 'It is trust and trust alone that must lead us to Love itself.'

In the next chapter we shall look more closely at the evolution of her spiritual journey.

❧ 2 ❧

'I Cannot Do It on My Own . . .'

LET US TRY TO IMAGINE a January evening in Lisieux in the year 1895. The brightest stars are apparent in the darkening sky. All is calm and peaceful in the town. The poor are warming themselves around wood-burning stoves, while middle-class families and friends are in their drawing-rooms busy with various social pursuits or exchanging news and gossip.

In the Carmelite convent close by, Thérèse has retired to the solitude of her cell. Her heavy habit gives her some protection from the cold. She is sitting on a small bench, which, together with a hard bed made from three planks, two trestles and a straw mattress, is all the furniture she has.

Not long before this, Thérèse celebrated her twenty-second birthday. She will soon enter her seventh year in the monastery. The adolescent has become a woman with the same enthusiasm as before, although now she is wiser and more inward-looking. She does not know that tuberculosis has already begun to destroy her lungs.

Tonight, however, Thérèse is happy. Her heart is over-flowing with peace and joy. Although it is very cold, the stark solitude of the evening has a festive quality, for the little room seems to radiate God's presence.

Thérèse has a small portable desk on her knees and is jotting down her childhood memories. She has been asked to do this by her sister Pauline – now Mother Agnes of Jesus and her prioress. To be sure, she had entertained a few doubts about the usefulness of this task and hesitated ever so briefly, but now she settles down to work.

What she wants to write about is not so much her 'life' as the role of her Beloved in her love adventure. She does not want to narrate a series of facts or events, but to talk about God's goodness to her and how his grace shines through everything that happens in her life. Her vocation, her suffering, her struggles, and her entire existence are characterized by the mystery of God's mercy:

> I find myself at a period in my life when I can cast a glance back on the past; my soul has matured in the crucible of exterior and interior trials. And now, like a flower strengthened by the storm, I can raise my head and see the words of Psalm 23 [22] realized in me: 'The Lord is my Shepherd, I shall not want; he makes me lie down in green pastures. He leads me beside still waters; he restores my soul. He leads me in paths of righteousness for his name's sake. Even though I walk through the valley of the shadow of death, I fear no evil; for thou art with me.' (A 3 r; Au 15)

Thérèse stops thinking along these lines for a while. The yellowish light of her kerosene lamp flutters gently on the bare walls of her cell. She starts to recall the past. Everything has happened so quickly. Her memories seem to unfold before her as if projected on a cinema screen.

The School of Suffering

Thérèse sees herself entering Carmel, her 'desert', on 9 April 1888. She is incredibly happy and all the sisters are there to welcome her, but behind them another, invisible, presence also greets her – Jesus on the cross:

> Yes, suffering opened wide its arms to me and I threw myself into them with love. ... When one wishes to attain a goal, one must use the means; Jesus made me understand that it was through suffering that he wanted to give me souls, and my attraction for suffering grew in proportion to its increase. This was my way for five years; exteriorly nothing revealed my suffering, which was all the more painful since I alone was aware of it. (A 69 v; Au 149)

What exactly did this long period of suffering consist of? Thérèse was not referring so much to the external sacrifices inherent in a cloistered life and which as an adolescent she would have found hard to bear, for she had accepted from the start, and even longed for, the physical solitude, meagre diet, curtailed sleep, lack of heat, and sparse furnishings. The opportunity to sacrifice something actual and tangible was very gratifying. A novice in her initial fervor would have experienced this chance to pay her spiritual dues, so to speak, as a stimulating incentive and, probably, as a useful introduction to the even more ascetic way of life that lay ahead of her. A novice would have expected an impressive outcome from the experience, which might well have produced a feeling of inward satisfaction and a sense of security when contemplating the long trek towards God. At the start, Thérèse shared the not uncommon desire to practice excessive mortification, but her superiors wisely forbade this. Nevertheless, we might well shudder in the present age when Thérèse declares that she suffered from the freezing winter nights in Normandy to 'the point of nearly dying from them' (PA 830).

The greater source of suffering Thérèse mentioned was certainly a matter of human relationships. It is not always easy to live constantly with others in such close confinement. On the contrary: rubbing elbows with the same people and looking at the same faces day after day throughout a lifetime is scarcely enjoyable. To select only one of many possible instances, consider how very difficult Thérèse found the experience of trying to confide in her mistress of novices, Sister Marie des Anges. Although Sister Marie was sweet-natured and always ready to offer good advice, Thérèse could not share the deepest aspirations of her soul with her, however hard she tried to do so. Then there was Sister Martha, one of Thérèse's novices, who was far from accommodating to begin with, and who seemed to enjoy opposing her at every turn. Her two sisters, Pauline and Marie, represented a trial of a different kind; Thérèse loved them dearly but neither wanted nor maintained a family relationship with them:

> I didn't come to Carmel to live with my sisters but to answer Jesus' call. Ah! I really felt in advance that this living with one's own sisters had to be the cause of continual suffering when one wishes to grant nothing to one's natural inclinations. (C 8 v; Au 216)

Above all others, there was Mother Marie de Gonzague, who, except for an interruption lasting three years, was Thérèse's prioress throughout her religious life. Mother Marie could be really charming, so charming indeed that Thérèse almost became attached to her. But the prioress was generally temperamental and touchy, and readily suspicious of the 'Martin clan', especially of the highly gifted Pauline (Sister Agnes), whose influence was starting to be felt in the community. The 'five years of suffering' Thérèse referred to earlier coincided exactly with her first five years under Mother Marie de Gonzague's priorship. As Thérèse remarked tactfully:

> Our Mother Prioress, frequently ill, had little time to spend with me. I know that she loved me very much and said everything good about me that was possible, nevertheless, God permitted that she was VERY SEVERE, *without her even being aware of it.* I was unable to meet her without having to kiss the floor, and it was the same thing on those rare occasions when she gave me spiritual direction. What an inestimable grace! How *visibly* God was acting within her who took his place! What would have become of me if I had been the 'pet' of the community as some of the Sisters believed? (A 70 v; Au 150)

In a later report to Mother Marie, Thérèse recalled her 'strict maternal training' (C 1 v). But it was usually the 'strict' aspect that was dominant and overshadowed Thérèse's everyday life. One day Thérèse admitted to another sister, 'I can assure you that I had many struggles and that I was not one day without suffering, not one!' (PA 1113).

Thérèse was not in the habit of complaining, however, and her reticence on the subject has disappointed many of her hagiographers. In this respect she usually, and almost mischievously, refers them to a disclosure in the hereafter: 'Everything that I have just written in a few words would require many pages of details but no one will ever read them in this life' (A 75 r).

Prayer: An Arduous Task

The hours of fervent mystical prayer Thérèse had practised

before entering Carmel probably intensified her longing for solitude. She looked forward to an undisturbed life with God in Carmel, where she would be free of any concern apart from the pursuit of love, and would exist in a contemplative atmosphere never broken by worldly intrusions.

But now things began to take a quite different turn. Her prayer life at home had been focused and consoling; now it was dry and full of distractions during the long hours in the convent chapel. 'Therefore, behold, I will allure her, and bring her into the wilderness, and speak tenderly to her' (Hosea 2: 14). Now that she found herself in that wilderness, the voice of her Beloved had somehow become almost silent. Thérèse admitted candidly: 'Dryness was my daily bread' (A 73 v); and: 'I should be distressed about sleeping (these last seven years) during my meditations and thanksgiving' (A 75 v). Her annual retreats were, if that were possible, 'even dryer' (A 76 r), and: 'Jesus slept in my little boat, as always' (A 79 v).

This unexpected situation was a harsh disappointment for a young Carmelite, the very nature of whose vocation required her to seek the Lord's presence at all times. As a result, she was quite disorientated. A novice often supposes that success in her prayer life is something like a barometer of her spiritual progress. Moreover, the examples of Teresa of Avila and John of the Cross, Thérèse's two great predecessors in Carmel, both of whom had been granted such immense mystical favors, must surely have made her seriously question the adequacy of her own generosity of spirit.

Objectively, of course, it would have been very unjust of Thérèse to attribute her dryness of spirit to any lack of 'fervor and fidelity' (A 75 v). Yet, if we consider what we know of her actual experience, her remark cannot be dismissed as a mere act of humility. Thérèse was well aware of her extreme spiritual poverty and had to learn to live with it. She also had to form new inward attitudes very patiently, and these labors were to last many years.

In time such trials bore fruit and contributed to the growth of her love and her desire to 'become little', like a grain of sand in the arid wilderness. They did not discourage her from loving but aroused her thirst for love: 'O God, thou art my God, I seek thee, my soul thirsts for thee; my flesh faints for thee, as in a dry and weary land where no water is' (Ps 63: 1). Thérèse's generosity began to enter a new dimension, for Jesus was teaching her 'the way to please him and to practice the sublimest virtues' (A 76 r).

Her humility and detachment, trust and abandonment took root and began to thrive. Thérèse learned to react to everything with versatility, now that her faith was fully active and her love totally disinterested:

> Today more than yesterday, if that were possible, I was deprived of all consolation. I thank Jesus, who finds this good for my soul, and . . . perhaps if he were to console me, I would stop at this sweetness, but he wants that all . . . be for himself! Well, then, all will be for Him, all, even when I feel I am able to offer nothing, so, just like this evening, I will give him this nothing! (LT 76; LC 101)

> If you only knew how great is my joy not to have anything with which to please Jesus! . . . It is a refined joy (but in no way felt). (LT 78; LC 105)

At last, after two and a half years in the novitiate, Thérèse was allowed to pronounce her religious vows on 8 September 1890. During the very dry retreat before the ceremony, she wrote her sister Pauline (Sister Agnes) a letter that offers a sure insight into her inward attitude on the threshold of her final declaration of commitment:

> . . . the little hermit must tell you the itinerary of her trip and here it is. Before she left, her Fiancé seemed to ask her in what country she desired to travel, what route she desired to follow, etc., etc. . . . The little fiancée answered that she had but one desire: that of being taken to the *summit of the mountain of Love*. To reach it many routes were offered to her, and there were so many perfect ones that she saw she was incapable of choosing. Then she said to her divine guide: 'You know where I want to go, you know for whom I want to climb the mountain, for whom I want to reach the goal. You know the one whom I love and the one whom I want to please solely; it is for him alone that I am undertaking this journey. Lead me, then, by the paths

which he loves to travel. I shall be at the height of my joy provided that he is pleased.' Then Jesus took me by the hand, and he made me enter a subterranean passage where it is neither hot nor cold, where the sun does not shine, and in which the rain or the wind does not visit, a subterranean passage where I see nothing but a half-veiled light, the light which was diffused by the lowered eyes of my Fiancé's Face! ... My Fiancé says nothing to me, and I say nothing to him either except that *I love Him more than myself*, and I feel at the bottom of my heart that it is true, for I am more his than my own. ... I don't see that we are advancing towards the summit of the mountain since our journey is being made underground, but it seems to me that we are approaching it without knowing how. The path on which I am has no consolation for me, and nevertheless it brings me all consolations since Jesus is the one who chose it, and I want to console him alone, alone! (LT 110; LC 132)

Thérèse's conviction that her faithful love would lead her to the summit of the mountain, even though she did not know exactly how this would happen, is impressive. The road would still be overshadowed by darkness, but now she knew that love meant taking the Lord's hand and letting him guide her.

At this point something definite was taking shape. Towards the end of 1894 the frequent practice of self-abandonment enabled Thérèse to produce the definitive version of her 'little way'. It was then that she sensed that the Lord was carrying her in his arms in order to raise her to the summit (C 3 r).

'The Greatest Cross That I Could Have Ever Imagined'

An even greater trial was bound to lead Thérèse to an increasing experience of abandonment. His youngest child reacted to the piteous mental and physical deterioration of Monsieur Martin as if to a sword piercing her heart.

Thérèse had barely entered Carmel when her father, then sixty-five, exhibited symptoms of the sickness to which he eventually succumbed. The mental results of arteriosclerosis and other afflictions were disastrous. Three months after Thérèse became a novice Monsieur Martin reached the point of total disorientation. One day he simply wandered off. His family went through anguish wondering where he might be and fearing the worst. His three daughters felt utterly helpless as they listened to the accounts of fruitless searches. Thérèse could only pray to her crucified Jesus. Four days later her father was traced to Le Havre.

A recurrence of his illness caused Thérèse's vesture ceremony to be postponed for a few months. At last he seemed to recover sufficiently to attend, and the presence of her deeply devout father at the ceremony on 10 January 1889 brought more light into Thérèse's somewhat somber world:

> The most beautiful, the most attractive flower of all was my dear King; never had he looked so handsome, so *dignified*! Everybody admired him. This was really his day of *triumph* and it was to be his last celebration on this earth. (A 72 r; Au 155)

But Monsieur Martin had not really recovered. Moreover, his financial affairs were almost in a shambles. He often talked such nonsense that his doctors, amateur psychiatrists at best, spread the suggestion that the departure of Thérèse, the apple of his eye, had caused his illness. Thérèse reacted sensitively to these 'pin-pricks' and suffered bitterly as the gossip spread. She wrote to Céline:

> Yes, ... Jesus is there with his cross! ... The things of this earth ... what do they mean to us? Should this be our homeland, this *slime*, so unworthy of an immortal soul? ... And what does it matter to us that cowardly men *harvest* the mustiness that grows on this slime? The more our heart is in heaven, the less we feel these *pin-pricks* ... for, then, our life is a *martyrdom*, and one day Jesus will give us the palm. To suffer and be despised ... what *bitterness* but what glory. (LT 81; LC 109)

But the end was not in sight. As his arteries hardened Monsieur Martin relapsed. As a result of an increasingly delusional state he armed himself with a revolver, and, one day in February, entrenched himself in a room in his house. The lives of Léonie and Céline, the two daughters still at home, and that of the maid-servant, were at risk until Isidore Guérin, his brother-in-law, arrived and, with a friend's help, disarmed

Monsieur Martin. He was sent immediately to a psychiatric institution in Caen and confined there.

Under the heading 'grace-filled days', Thérèse tells us that she considered 12 February 1889 to be their *great wealth*. But she found the day itself immensely painful:

> I didn't know that on February 12, a month after my reception of the Habit, our dear Father would drink the most bitter and most humiliating of all chalices. Ah! that day, I didn't say I was able to suffer more! Words cannot express our anguish, and I'm not going to attempt to describe it. (A 73 r; Au 157)

It would not be too fanciful to say that Thérèse drank from that same chalice, and to the very dregs.

Thérèse, the grain of sand, felt trampled under foot, humiliated and crushed, like her father. Her noble 'king' was apparently insane and, in the manner of the times, the laughing-stock of the town. His family was not spared similar treatment, for public opinion in those days was more cruel than sympathetic to people suffering from what we would now classify as specific psychiatric syndromes. Moreover, Thérèse would certainly have known something of the methods of forced treatment then in use. She would have pictured her father's isolation in the mental institution, and speculated on the type of care he was receiving from complete strangers. She would have considered the problem of his five daughters' inability to alleviate his suffering. Thérèse's own cup of sorrow was surely full and overflowing.

Fifteen days later she wrote: 'Jesus is a Spouse of Blood. He wants for himself all the blood of one's heart' (LT 82); 'That cross was the greatest cross that I could have ever imagined' (LT 155).

Monsieur Martin survived for more than three years in the Caen institution. A few months after his internment, 'Les Buissonnets' was emptied and sold to new proprietors. Nothing remained of Thérèse's childhood there.

I believe that yet another struggle, profoundly connected with her relationship with her father, can be discerned between the lines of Thérèse's writings: her perplexity about God himself. What had just happened to father, family and home was too disconcerting and disorientating for her sensitive nature.

Her experience of a good, devout and wise father was a major element in the concept of God that she had developed as a child and held until then. For her, Papa was an icon of God himself. As a child she 'needed but to look at him to know how the saints pray' (A 18 r). She would observe how 'during his daily visits to the Blessed Sacrament his eyes would fill with tears and his face would reflect celestial bliss' (A 71 v). She had just written to him from Carmel: 'When I think of you, my darling little father, I naturally think of God' (LT 58). But suddenly Monsieur Martin was saying and doing things so utterly foolish, incoherent, and even irrational that her notion of him as a mirror of God fell and broke into a thousand pieces. This also made her tend to think of God as entirely other, strange and incomprehensible.

This sixteen-year-old adolescent now had to confront her 'mystery'. Under the extreme weight of her suffering, a young thinker like Thérèse, living in the solitude of a convent, turned her mind to key metaphysical questions, even though she tried to suppress such thoughts. Why did God who was so good allow such things to happen? Was it fair to let these things happen to someone who had always served him so faithfully (shades of Job whose questions would not be stilled), especially when she had prayed so much, and with such fervour, and such trust? If prayer could be followed by such events and phenomena, did God respond to it anyway? Of course, many people, including Thérèse, often and emphatically insisted that suffering was a privilege for those whom God particularly loved, and that everything would be rewarded and compensated for in heaven. But was there a heaven anyway?

It is not inconceivable that such a question could have occurred to Thérèse. Anyway, something very like that would come to her mind with particular intensity in the last two years of her life, at a time when she had become an exceptionally strong believer. Nevertheless, in her autobiography, she all but omitted this period of her father's stay in the mental hospital. All the same, one significant statement in this respect did escape her, quite inadvertently: 'I was then having great trials of all kinds (to the point of asking myself sometimes if there was a Heaven)' (A 80 v).

Her letters show how very defensive she became. Her vocabulary seems exceedingly combative. She is more inclined than ever before to affirm her faith, without seeing or understanding, and declares herself ready for any suffering as a follower of Jesus. Her letters reveal many 'irritations', but that was inevitable. It was a difficult time for her; yet, in spite of her youth – she was seventeen – she realized the need to fight on and, amid considerable pain and suffering, gradually recovered from 'the great blow'.

Jesus 'learned obedience through his sufferings', and Thérèse learned to mature in the same 'crucible' (A 3 r). Rare flowers can emerge from a swamp. In Thérèse's case, flowers of humility, detachment, confidence and abandonment were sure to blossom in that good ground. But for the moment prayer was needed more than ever in order to cope with so very personal a trial. Later, when she looked back at this period of her life, Thérèse wrote:

> Yes, Papa's three years of martyrdom appear to me as the most lovable, the most fruitful of my life; I wouldn't exchange them for all the ecstasies and revelations of the saints. My heart overflows with gratitude when I think of this inestimable *treasure* that must cause a holy jealousy to the angels of the heavenly court. (A 73 r; Au 157)

Thérèse's New Perception of God

From a theological standpoint, Thérèse's growth was astonishing. Now that her former concept of God had been shattered, she discerned the true reflection of God, that of Jesus as the Father's Envoy, much more intensely and explicitly than in the past.

Jesus, the risen Lord, had to suffer first. Thérèse discovered the 'Holy Face' of the Lord during her great period of trial. As if she had had a presentiment of this discovery, on the day of her vesture she had added the words 'and of the Holy Face' to the name she had already adopted. Henceforth, her ideal of imitation of and resemblance to her suffering Lord would become the basic tie binding her to him for ever. He taught her how far love and fidelity could take her. Two months after her father's commitment to the Caen psychiatric home, Thérèse wrote to Céline to describe more explicitly how she surveyed 'the depths of the hidden treasures of the Holy Face ... the mysteries of love hidden in the Face of the Spouse' (A 71 r):

> To be the spouse of Jesus, we *must* resemble Jesus, and Jesus is all bloody, he is crowned with thorns! ... Look at his eyes lifeless and lowered! Look at his wounds! ... Look at Jesus in his face. ... There you will see how he loves us. (LT 87; LC 110)

> Yes, the Face of Jesus is *luminous*, but if in the midst of wounds and tears it is already so beautiful, what will it be, then, when we behold it in heaven? oh, heaven ... heaven. (LT 95; LC 114)

In the summer of 1890 she quoted for the first time, and at great length, chapters 53 and 63 of Isaiah, which talk of 'the hidden face of the Man of Sorrows who bore our pains', who 'alone trampled the winepress as he looked about for someone to help him' (LT 108).

Thérèse became increasingly receptive to the message of the Bible. Jesus had become not only her ideal and her love but her truth and *raison d'être*. Thérèse was baptized and raised in the Christian faith, which was confirmed by her home instruction and nourished by reading, especially by the *Imitation of Christ* and Arminjon's *The End of the Present World and the Mysteries of the Future Life*. But during her father's illness she entered a third phase in her spiritual development: the passage from a traditional faith to a personal faith duly accepted and assumed with all its responsibilities.

It was only to be expected that when Thérèse was confronted with others' and her own suffering, the great metaphysical questions facing all human beings should arise for her too. Of course she did not examine them systematically. Nevertheless, the nature of the trials she had to endure at that time made it inevitable that such questions would arise in perhaps the remotest corners of her mind, even though she probably erased them just as quickly by recourse to currently acceptable answers. All the same, because she was fundamentally a 'thinker', Thérèse's response to faith, which until then had been whole-hearted but far from conceptual and speculative, now became personal and conscious. It was no longer automatic. Such words as 'seek', 'find' and 'understand' flowed from her very easily (they were used 46, 137 and 144 times respectively in her autobiography alone). Thérèse possessed a lively, critical intelligence, on which she drew directly only now. Some people would say that her Norman ancestry meant that her realistic mind required a serious foundation before it would accept anything supernatural.

'We live in an age of inventions', she wrote later (C 2 v). Hasty generalizations did not interest her. She noted how futile the vague answers to which she so objected could be. Shortly before her death, she told Pauline: 'It's the reasoning of the worst materialistic minds that would impress itself on mine.' With foresight she declared: 'Later on, from continually making new advances, science will explain everything naturally and will be the answer to everything that exists and still remains a problem, for there are many things to be discovered, etc.'

Before her sixteenth birthday, she had 'not yet found the treasures hidden in the Gospel' (A 47 r). But a few years later she wrote: 'In the Gospels I find everything necessary for my poor little soul. I'm always finding in them new lights, new meanings both hidden and mysterious' (A 83 v).

She was firmly rooted in the Gospels and Epistles. She understood them intuitively, and was instinctively aware, for example, that these earliest witnesses, intelligent and discerning men such as Matthew, Luke, John and Paul (and, as Jews, all monotheists), could have believed in Jesus as Lord and Son of God only if their motivation was utterly compelling. Thérèse always responded very sensitively to Jesus' powerful signs and epiphanies, and referred to them constantly in her writings. Of course she reacted most emphatically to the most effective of all the testimonies offered by God the Father: the resurrection of Jesus, which she saw as the ultimate divine confirmation of the seriousness of his message. A year before she died Thérèse even composed a personal concordance of accounts of the resurrection. Certainly she may be said to have 'studied' the New Testament assiduously.

Thérèse was an honest seeker after truth: 'Jesus, you know that I seek the truth' (B 4 v). A few hours before her death she said: 'Yes, it seems to me that I have sought nothing but the truth' (DE 205). Thérèse would always listen sincerely and serenely to whatever was said in the name of Jesus. If an answer was required, she accepted full responsibility and provided it to the limit of her capabilities as she understood them: 'To love is to give everything. It's to give oneself' (PN 54).

Nevertheless, the truth did not prevent her from falling into the night of the senses for, like so many saints before her, she experienced the darkness of faith, although she remained unfailingly loyal to that faith. Through the hours of darkness and the raging of all the tempests that assailed her, she held to the reality of Jesus, her support whole and entire: 'I am running to my Jesus' (C 7 r).

When she wrote those words, her soul was already replete with experience of Jesus' reality and activity there. Given that experience, she was so bound to him that she could no longer leave him. During her father's illness, however, she had not yet received sufficient divine confirmation of what the reality of the Lord was to mean in and for her to allow that specific assurance. Nevertheless, she was on the right road to its affirmation in herself. In her overwhelming sadness and grief she had discerned the Face of Jesus, and from then on she regularly contemplated its meaning for her. She began to realize what it meant to say that the Father had not spared his beloved Son suffering and death. Thérèse no longer thought of the incomprehensible mystery of death as absurd or incompatible with the Father's goodness. Jesus became her great defence, and his word her main assurance. She would never pretend to know better than Jesus. From now on her faith would be authentically Christian in the sense of Christ-based.

Thérèse is a very interesting personality for our times because she was quite aware of the questions we ask and found the answers to them. But a thousand questions and a thousand temptations do not constitute a single real doubt. She never let go of Jesus' guiding hand. Later, when she described her personal 'dark night of the soul', she used such obviously relevant metaphors as 'storm', 'darkness', 'struggle', 'torment', 'trial', 'tunnel', 'fog', 'night', 'wall', and even 'temptation', but she never referred to 'doubt'. When she applied her intellect to a problem, this did not imply any doubt that God would proffer an answer or solution to it. She had become 'supernaturally' detached from any such possibility. Thérèse never rebelled, in any real sense. Instead, she found in God and in her faith in him a 'peace ... which never abandoned me in the midst of the greatest trials' (A 69 v). But, she added: 'He who says peace does not mean joy, or at least *felt* joy'.

As Christians, we do not necessarily have to undergo the same trial of faith as Thérèse. But this does not mean that we should not try to discern and seek out the 'why' of suffering in the midst of our own tribulations. We can rely on the words of Jesus, and also find support in those of Mary, or of truly exceptional saints like Thérèse. We can also have recourse to the faith of the church community, including the assurance of believers who have gone before us. That is one of the blessings offered us by the Church. 'I love the Church', Thérèse used to say (B 4 v). As we make our own personal journey to God we can surely profit from it and from the light that others have received in and through it.

An Impossible Task

This young girl in her mid-teens was not only becoming a strong believer but was already passionately devoted to the Lord. When she loved someone, she gave herself totally.

When Thérèse left home, she had a very clear objective: 'I want to be a saint. The other day I read words that appealed to me very much. I don't recall the saint who said them; they were "I am not perfect, but *I want* to be perfect"' (LT 45). She underlined 'I want'.

To become a 'saint', 'a great saint': this was a refrain that she repeated very often in the early letters of her religious life. The prioress, Mother Marie de Gonzague, referred to Thérèse's patron saint when she advised her thus: 'You must become a second St Teresa!' and helped the intention to become quite resolute. Thérèse was not slow to tell Céline, still at home, about her convictions:

> What [Céline] does not know perhaps is the love that Jesus has for her, a love that demands ALL. There is nothing that is impossible for him. He does not want to set any limit to his lily's SANCTITY. His limit is that there is no limit! ... We are greater than the whole universe, and one day we *ourselves* shall have a divine existence. (LT 83; LC 109)

What did it mean to become a saint? How could Thérèse conceive of it otherwise than as an unconditional Yes to the most radical demands of love, whatever they turned out to be? Once again she disclosed the inclinations of her heart in a letter to Céline: 'Jesus asks for *everything* from you, *everything*, *everything*, as much as He can ask of the great saints' (LT 57). She underscored 'everything' two, three and five times respectively.

Did she really know what it meant to give everything? Naturally, any generous soul might decide on an agenda of that kind in a moment of fervent enthusiasm, but when faced with love's constant and unrelenting demands for evidence of personal sincerity, anyone, even the future St Thérèse of Lisieux, would soon tend to feel poor and inadequate, for Jesus did not come to bring peace but the sword (Matt. 10: 34) and a daily cross (Luke 9: 23). No disciple is above the master (Matt. 10: 24), who was filled with anguish and bathed in a bloody sweat at the thought of his impending passion and death (Luke 22: 44).

Was Thérèse really aware of the implications of her temerity in uttering these sentiments:

> It is incredible how big my heart appears to me when I consider all earth's treasures. ... But when I consider Jesus, how little it appears to me! ... I would so much like to love him! ... Love him more than he has ever been loved! (LT 74; LC 100)

Could Thérèse have been aiming at a kind of world record (so to speak) in loving God? That might seem to be the case, for she intended to equal the achievements in loving of St Teresa of Avila, and, if possible, to improve upon them – which was scarcely a modest objective as far as emulation of singularly holy individuals is concerned! But if we think of Thérèse's weakness, the comparison that comes immediately to mind is with David's encounter with the giant Goliath, when the inspired astuteness of David made up for his lack of physical strength.

Shortly after the foregoing, when in the midst of an especially difficult trial, Thérèse became acutely aware of her limitations. For the time being, she still saw her weaknesses and failures as 'surplus' suffering, and as a kind of privilege that allowed her to love God even more humbly and intensely, which does not mean that her love for him was qualitatively or quantitatively reduced, but that it was more realistic. She had neither lowered her sights nor modified the ideal state at which she aimed, even though her letters from the novitiate reveal her increasing awareness of her weakness:

> What a grace when, in the morning, we feel no courage, no strength to practice virtue; that is the moment to put the axe to the root of the tree. Instead of wasting our time gathering a few baubles, we can dip into diamonds, and what a profit at the end of the day. (LT 65; LC 88)

> ... the little lamb really must borrow from you a little strength and courage, that courage which makes the Lion surmount all things. (LT 75; LC 101)

She claimed that she was 'weakness itself' (LT 74). Yet to be weak was an authentic commendation in her eyes:

> You would like your heart to be a flame that rises up to him without the lightest smoke. Don't forget that the smoke that surrounds you is only for yourself in order to remove from you the sight of your love for Jesus. ... At least, then, he has this love entirely, for if he were to show it to us just a little bit, swiftly self-love would come like a fatal wind which extinguishes everything. (LT 81; LC 109)

> What an unspeakable joy to carry our crosses *feebly* (LT 82; LC 109)

A number of important things had now become clear to her:

> Let us not think that we can love without suffering, without suffering much. ... Our poor nature is there! and it isn't there for nothing! Our nature is our riches, our means of earning our bread! ... Let us suffer the bitter pain, without courage! (Jesus suffered in *sadness*! Without sadness, would the soul suffer?) ... Céline! what an illusion! ... We'd never want to fall? What does it matter, my Jesus, if I fall at each moment; *I see* my weakness through this, and this is a great gain for me. ... (LT 89; LC 111)

At the end of two and a half years of religious life as a novice, shortly before her profession, she admitted:

> You are mistaken ... if you believe that your little Thérèse walks always with fervor on the road of virtue. She is weak and very weak, and every day she has a new experience of this weakness, but ... Jesus is pleased to teach her, as he did St. Paul, the science of rejoicing in her infirmities. This is a great grace, and I beg Jesus to teach it to you, for peace and quiet of heart are to be found there only. (LT 109; LC 130)

Under Great Tension

The high ideal Thérèse had aspired to reach by her own means meant that she had set herself a formidable task. Thérèse neither could nor would allow anything to elude her loving attentiveness, and her concern about the smallest things became even more marked. During her canonization process, all the Sisters stressed her meticulously vigilant obedience to even the least important regulation, and to every wish expressed by Mother Marie de Gonzague, even though Mother Marie herself would forget all about it a few days later. Had Thérèse not been driven by burning love, all this would have seemed over-scrupulous and even obsessive. In her letters she often uses terms that reveal her exceptional concern for little everyday things and their unique value: a 'tear', 'sigh', 'look', 'bit of straw' or 'pin-prick': '... let us profit from the briefest moments, let us act like misers, let us be jealous of the smallest things for the Beloved!' (LT 101).

The folly of Jesus' love had to be paid for similarly:

> Jesus' love for Céline can be understood only by Jesus! ... Jesus has done foolish things for Céline. ... Let Céline do foolish things for Jesus. ... Love is repaid by love alone, and the wounds of love are healed only by love. (LT 85; LC 109)

For the time being, Thérèse banished the word 'impossible' from her vocabulary:

> Love can do all things, and the most difficult things don't appear difficult to it. Jesus does not look so much at the grandeur of actions or even their difficulty as at the love which goes to make up these actions. (LT 65; LC 88)

It was not 'what' we did but 'how' and 'why' we did it that determined the value of

> ... our poor, weak, insignificant love. ... It is true that sometimes we momentarily disdain gathering our treasures ... but in a single act of love, even *unfelt*, all is atoned for. (*ibid.*)

Thérèse also believed that love and suffering would grow together: 'The more her lily thrives in love, the more also it must thrive in suffering' (LT 83).

When she was nine and had just read about the heroic acts of Joan of Arc, Thérèse began to conceive of the call to holiness as a great adventure, and the ideal of martyrdom became part of her world. She had a presentiment that she too 'was born to glory', but that her 'glory would not appear to mortal eyes, that it would consist in becoming a great saint' (A 32 r). Thérèse always thought of Joan of Arc, not yet canonized at that time, as a kindred spirit. Joan was her choice of subject for two of the plays she was asked to write for her community's entertainment. The possibility of martyrdom was: 'the dream of my youth. That dream has grown with me under the cloisters of Carmel' (B 3 r). 'Our martyrdom is beginning', she wrote in her first letter after her father's commitment to the institution in Caen. 'Together let us enter the arena' (LT 82); and: 'I would rather die than abandon the glorious battlefield where the love of Jesus has placed me' (LT 83).

With anti-clericalism very strong in France in the late nineteenth century, some kind of persecution of the Church was a serious possibility, but Thérèse did not intend to wait for any such public campaign: 'Before dying by the sword, let us die by means of pin-pricks' (LT 86). 'The hidden martyrdom, known but to God ... martyrdom without honor, without triumph – *that* is love pushed to heroism' (LT 94).

Thérèse's gaze was intently yet lovingly fixed on the Suffering Servant of Yahweh, and she 'thirsted to suffer and to be forgotten' (A 71 r). Like her spiritual guide, St John of the Cross, she chose 'suffering and contempt here below as her only portion' (A 73 v). If life, as Teresa of Avila put it, was 'but a night spent in a miserable inn', then her spiritual descendant and namesake from Lisieux thought it more advisable to lodge in 'a hotel *entirely* bad than in one only half bad' (LT 49). The resulting aim, then, was 'to suffer and yet again and always, to suffer' (LT 81).

At this time, of course, suffering might be said to have worn a halo, for it was thought to be spiritually meritorious almost in itself. Three months after the Caen events, Thérèse even defined holiness as a loving and determined will to suffer: 'Holiness does not consist in saying pretty things, not even in thinking or feeling them! ... It consists in *suffering* and suffering from *everything*.' She appealed to Father Pichon's authority: 'Holiness! One must conquer it at sword point, one must suffer ... one must agonize ...' (LT 89).

Surely all the unpleasantness that the Martin sisters had to endure as a result of their beloved father's humiliating illness was a unique opportunity to undergo valuable holy suffering?

What a privilege Jesus grants us in sending such a great *sorrow*. ... He is giving us his favors just as he gave them to the greatest saints. ... Now we have no longer anything to hope for on earth, no longer anything but suffering and again suffering. When we have finished, suffering will still be there, extending its arm to us. Oh! What a lot worthy of envy! (LT 83; LC 109)

In her simplicity Thérèse believed that holiness depended on suffering, and therefore, ultimately, on her. It was necessary to 'master the art of suffering . . . at sword point', and to pay for it with one's blood. Every particle of suffering was a form of sacred currency: something like a gold piece that could be used to buy the fine jewelery of personal holiness. There were numberless appropriate occasions to make such acquisitions. Thérèse saw herself in her own situation as 'surrounded by immense riches' (LT 81). Their recent trials and tribulations comprised a 'gold mine to be exploited' (LT 82). Then Thérèse would recall the advice Marie used to give her little sister when they were both at home:

> I can still hear you saying to me: 'Look at the merchants, how much trouble they go to in order to earn money, and we can gather treasures for heaven at each moment without giving ourselves any trouble; we have only to gather diamonds with a RAKE.' And I went off, my heart filled with joy, filled with good resolutions! Without you, perhaps I'd not be in Carmel! (LT 91; LC 112)

Daughter of Two Entrepreneurs

In order to understand the direction Thérèse's spiritual life would take, we must remember that Thérèse was the child of two small business people. Her father had owned a successful jewelery and watch-maker's shop for twenty years. Her mother had run a lucrative lace-making business in her own home. Consequently, earning money, doing business, keeping the books and making investments were all commercial activities that were typical of Thérèse's milieu. Inevitably, like her older sisters had been before her, she was well used to such an atmosphere.

The Martins, however, were entrepreneurs not only in the world of affairs but in that of the spirit. Thérèse's education as a child was necessarily marked by a constant preoccupation with earning, saving and registering everything of monetary value. Under her sisters' influence, this preoccupation was carried over into her spiritual formation. No doubt it had some very positive effects. Such considerations were sure to encourage her generosity, for example, as well as her energy and her spiritual progress. The 'do-it-yourself' or self-sufficiency attitude encouraged in her at a time when she was already determined and naturally ambitious was certainly taken over into her spiritual life. In her judgement, therefore, nothing was insignificant: whether, as when aged four, she was already making and recording small voluntary sacrifices, or later on, when she anticipated Pauline, her teacher, giving her well-deserved prizes for success in her studies: 'There, as always, fairness was observed and I received only the rewards I deserved.' The subsequent association of ideas (with, in fact, the awesome Day of Judgement and the allocation of just rewards for war efforts) is very telling: 'My heart would beat so hard when I received the prizes and the crown – It was for me like a foretaste of Judgment Day' (A 19 v).

Later, when Pauline departed to the convent, Marie continued where the other had left off with Thérèse's education. Her elder sister prepared Thérèse, then eleven, for her First Communion:

> I sat on her lap and listened eagerly to everything she said to me. . . . Just as famous warriors taught their children the art of war, so Marie spoke to me about life's struggles and of the palm given to the victors. She spoke also about the eternal riches that one can so easily amass each day, and what a misfortune it was to pass by without so much as stretching forth one's hand to take them. (A 33 r; Au 74)

The means used are important:

> She explained the way of becoming holy through fidelity in little things; furthermore, she gave me a little leaflet called 'Renunciation' and I meditated on this with delight. (*ibid.*)

Thérèse's family environment had certainly acquainted her with the imagery of becoming rich as if one were some kind of spiritual merchant, and with considering the smallest details of the procedure with the precision and care of a watch-maker and the meticulous refinement of a lace-maker.

Although now in the convent, Pauline also took a hand in

the instruction process. She compiled a prettily decorated notebook, covering the ten weeks leading to Thérèse's First Communion, with a short prayer and a flower symbol for each day. To prepare herself for the solemn event Thérèse had to recite the prayer frequently and make a great number of minor sacrifices symbolized by the flower. She had to record each one in her notebook and offer them all to Jesus on the day itself. Thérèse was delighted:

> You don't know the joy I felt when Marie showed me your pretty little book. I found it delightful. I had never seen anything so beautiful and I was unable to grow tired looking at it. ... Every day I try to perform as many practices as I can, and I do all in my power not to let a single occasion pass by. I am saying all the little prayers which form the perfume of roses, as often as I can. (LT 11; LC 28)

The results were scarcely negligible. The sixty-eight days of preparation brought 1,949 small sacrifices: that is, 27 a day; and 2,773 short prayers: or 40 a day.

The importance of good deeds and of perseverance in good works was also stressed at the abbey school where Thérèse was enrolled at the time. In her notebook of retreat sermons when preparing for her First Communion, Thérèse remarked: 'I promised myself to make real efforts to be good and to have many good deeds to offer to God.'

Now let us return to Carmel, the school of suffering where Thérèse was now enrolled. It was more important than ever to make good use of all that Marie had taught her. Just before entering Carmel she had reminded herself yet again:

> I desire only one thing when I am in Carmel ... it is always to suffer for Jesus. Life passes so quickly that truly it must be better to have a truly beautiful crown and a little trouble than (not) to have an ordinary one without any trouble. ... (LT 43; LC 75)

Her vigilance was constant, even extreme: 'For a Carmelite, a day spent without suffering is a day wasted' (LT 54); and: 'The grain of sand, despite its littleness, wants to fashion a beautiful eternity for itself, and also for the souls of sinners' (LT 54).

'To struggle much, to suffer much, to accumulate spiritual riches!' These expressions recurred throughout the first year of Thérèse's religious life. They were often combative, sometimes painful, and frequently characterized by a sense of the practical: 'One can't suffer too much to win the palm of victory' (LT 55). A phrase indicating urgency would usually follow: '... time passes quickly, I see it slipping by me with frightening speed' (LT 62). The conclusion was: 'Let us hurry to fashion our crown ...' (LT 94).

Thérèse's ideal was so lofty and difficult to attain that her love would always be running ahead, as it were, and so much so that she barely touched the ground. That is why she reproached herself so often for her littleness, tepidity and everyday weakness. Thérèse had to mature inwardly and be purified before she could rejoice to find herself before God with empty hands. Only then would she understand that she would receive God as an act of his mercy, and not as a result of her own fidelity to grace.

Questions of Conscience

But Thérèse also possessed a very delicate conscience. Her soul was profoundly affected by even the very least fault, which could provoke numberless anxious doubts about her integrity. Her particular psychology included a highly refined sensibility that was immeasurably heightened by her unique soul-life. For instance, as a child she had stayed awake the whole night pondering the possibility that God was not entirely happy about the events of her day. Later on this acute sensitivity would degenerate into anguish and scruples about her developing affections and frustration at her own supposed inadequacies. A complete lack of sexual instruction during puberty was another reason for very real inner turmoil (A 39 r; 44 r).

In addition, once she had passed through these major crises, hidden qualms still had to be dealt with. Thérèse paid a heavy tribute to the morality of her day, which so easily imputed grievous sin to a person and situation wholly devoid of any such thing. Accordingly, she was immensely relieved when, shortly after she entered Carmel, Father Pichon assured her that she had never committed a single mortal sin. 'But,' he added, 'if God were to abandon you, you'd become a little devil instead of a little angel.' 'Ah, I had no trouble believing it', said Thérèse, even then, for: 'I felt how weak and imperfect I was.'

The reason for her torment seems very odd indeed when we first encounter it: 'I had such a great fear of having tarnished my baptismal robe' (LT 70). The fear in question was not so much, or only, a matter of being in an actual state of sin as one of honour with regard to her absolute fidelity in the past. This was a kind of 'noblesse oblige' attitude that impelled her to keep her 'coat of arms' perfectly dust-free and immaculate. Thérèse had to be irreproachable in God's eyes and, ultimately, in her own. She had to be perfected, 'finished' in God's eyes, and impeccable, in order to win her self-approval. Of course we cannot fail to be struck by the less than subtle note of self-gratification and complacency in Thérèse's ambition here. Her condition here is still a long way from the 'line of conduct' she would eventually adopt and follow to the summit of personal spiritual maturity. When she reached that point every glance at herself dissolved under the scrutiny of God's infinite mercy:

> If I had committed all possible crimes, I would always have the same confidence; I feel that this whole multitude of offenses would be like a drop of water thrown into a fiery furnace. (DE 89)

Thérèse had a great number of difficulties to contend with in regard to the nature and implication of sinning. Sister Agnes (Pauline) testified that the fear of offending God 'poisoned' (PO 1513) Thérèse's existence at the beginning of her religious life. Of course, she was human and did commit faults, but they were all very minor things. Nevertheless, the Jansenistic mentality of the times meant that these tiny imperfections were severely judged and subject to reprimands. For example, when Thérèse went to Confession and accused herself of an inability to stay awake during Mass, the confessor and chaplain, Father Prou, lectured her sternly and convinced her that she had offended the Almighty. The other nuns did not fare any better. One day he succeeded in 'encouraging' one of them by saying: 'My poor child, all I can tell you is that you already have one foot in hell and that, if you continue like this, you'll soon have the other one there too!' Fortunately the prioress, Mother Marie de Gonzague, consoled the poor girl thus: 'Don't worry, my own two feet are already there' (LT 112, note e).

Thérèse's extreme concern about being pure beyond all reproach gradually relaxed as she became aware of the degree of indulgence in God's judgements. A letter written a few days before her profession makes this clear:

> Tell him, too, to take me on the day of my Profession if I must still offend him afterwards. . . . But it seems to me that Jesus can give me the grace of no longer offending him or committing faults that DON'T OFFEND him but serve only to humble and to make love much stronger. (LT 114; LC 137)

A little over a year after her profession on 8 September 1890, she met Father Prou during the annual retreat. The retreat-master assured her that her faults 'did not grieve' the Lord. Thérèse said she had never contemplated that possibility, even remotely. Thus Father Prou '. . . launched her in full sail on the waves of *trust* and of *love*' (A 80 v).

In spite of the liberating effect of this assurance, Thérèse did not always manage to embark without care or anguish on the ocean of God's understanding love. Fifteen months later, Father Pichon had to reassure her most emphatically:

> No, no, you have not committed any mortal sin. I swear it. No, one cannot sin grievously without knowing it. No, after absolution has been granted, one must not doubt one's state of grace. So banish all your worries. God wants it so and I order you to do so. Believe on my word: Never, never, never have you committed a single mortal sin. (20 Jan. 1893; LC 151, conflated)

Thérèse Resigns Herself

At the start Thérèse certainly believed that she would ascend the mountain route to the summit of holiness if she could only

exert herself with the appropriate degree of ardor. She still did
not understand that only the sanctifying 'arms' of Jesus would
bear her to that summit. Admittedly, Thérèse did use the term
'arms' in that respect in her letters, but she also contemplated
the possibility that Jesus could leave her behind. But surely that
would not be a problem in the end, for her poverty would act as
a trump card as far as her humility and thus her love were
concerned (LT 89). Later, however, her viewpoint changed:
Jesus would surely take her up and carry her to the heights
above. He must do so, for there was no other way for her to get
there. Left to her own devices, she would remain but an
'obscure grain of sand', and holiness would be 'a mountain
whose summit was lost in the clouds' (C 2 v).

During her first years in Carmel, the conviction that 'I
cannot become a saint on my own, it is beyond my strength!'
took hold of her and gradually matured. But the desire she
expressed on the day of her profession, 'Infinite love, without
limit other than yourself', had become not merely a lofty but a
superhuman task!

Thérèse noticed that she still quite often committed faults in
'small things'. She had to face up to her powerlessness. But the
Beloved became ever more lovable and the ideal of requited
love increasingly sublime. Yet how can we poor creatures ever
manage to do anything appropriate in return for what God has
done for us? How can we rival him? How (as it were) can we
get even with him? Thérèse's notion of God was evolving more
rapidly than the strength of her heart. Her meditation on the
Bible and the works of St John of the Cross gave her an acute
sense of the infinite worth of the All-Holy, of the Absolute
Being who is gratuitous Love. This vision aroused her to a
strong conviction of personal insufficiency. She would have to
experience a disruption and shattering of the construction that
was her beautiful dream of her love (her own love, that is), but
then, on the resulting ruins God would build *his* dream for
Thérèse.

Up to the present that insufficiency had been an obstacle to
be overcome. But now, slowly, she was learning to integrate the
way of abandonment into her everyday life. Under the burden
of her former spiritual course, the will to generate perfect love

gradually receded into the background and gave way to God's own initiative. The 'I-You' relationship underwent an inversion and became 'You-I'. The determined attitude of 'I want to do it and I will do it for you' became much more peaceful and trusting: 'I cannot do it myself, therefore you will do it for me.'

Thérèse became aware of her spiritual poverty with some difficulty and even a few crises. But this problematical course was her way of learning to accept what was necessary. Holiness would no longer be something to be achieved by her own actions but a gift from God. Now she would learn definitively to surrender to God's grace, the only form of grace that makes anyone authentically holy. By the end of 1894 that would prove to be the great turning-point in her spiritual life. Before looking more closely at that decisive time of change, however, it is necessary to examine the events of 1893 and 1894 in greater detail.

Release Through Abandonment

In 1893, when Thérèse was twenty years old and had almost five years of religious life behind her, the community underwent a radical change. Sister Agnes (Pauline) replaced Mother Marie de Gonzague as prioress. An authoritarian, sometimes harsh, form of rule was replaced by the direction of Thérèse's second mother. She wrote:

> My nature was such that fear made me recoil; with *love*, not only did I advance, I actually *flew*. ... Oh, Mother, it was especially since the blessed day of your election that I have flown in the ways of love. ... On that day Pauline became my living Jesus. (A 80 v; Au 174)

In addition, Monsieur Martin, though paralysed and presumably suffering from dementia, had been back with his family since 10 May of the previous year. To some extent, now that the grief and shame of 'Caen' were in the past, time healed the wounds of that experience.

Thérèse was now living in a much more tolerable psychological atmosphere. As her external suffering decreased and she became more aware of her own powerlessness, her dream of 'littleness', even of being something as minute as a grain of sand, also changed substantially. From now on Thérèse was less inclined to demean herself openly in others' eyes and tried to become poorer in her own eyes. Her new plan of action was to aim at nothing that inflated her ego even secretly, and to relinquish all rights of ownership, even her right to love of self.

After her private retreat in 1892, Thérèse wrote to Céline and described the new insights that were about to demonstrate their value and importance:

> Jesus tells us [as he did Zacchaeus] to descend. . . . Where then must we descend? . . . Céline, you know better than I, however, let me tell you where we must now follow Jesus. In days gone by, the Jews asked our divine Savior: 'Master, where do you live?' And he answered: 'The foxes have their lairs, the birds of heaven their nests, but I have no place to rest my head.' This is where we must descend in order that we may serve as an abode for Jesus. To be so poor that we do not have a place to rest our head. This is, dear Céline, what Jesus has done in my soul during my retreat. . . . You understand, I am speaking here of the interior. Besides, has not the exterior already been reduced to nothing by means of the very sad trial of Caen? . . . In our dear Father, Jesus has stricken us in the most sensitive exterior part of our heart; now let us allow him to act. He can complete his work in our souls. . . . What Jesus desires is that we receive him into our hearts. No doubt, they are already empty of creatures, but, alas, I feel mine is not entirely empty of myself, and it is for this reason that Jesus tells me to descend. . . . He, the King of kings, humbled himself in such a way that his face was hidden, and no one recognized him . . . and I, too, want to hide my face, I want my Beloved alone to see it, that he may be the only one to count my tears . . . that in my heart at least he may rest his dear head and feel that there he is known and understood! (LT 137)

She was now more resolute than ever before in her desire to renounce all the claims of egotism and her longing to 'disappear completely'. This resolution was now concentrated on the most personal and intimate level of her psyche. This was quite normal in a generous-hearted seeker after God who, after years of spiritual struggle with pride and self-love in the subtle refinements proper to her, had come to understand them more proficiently. From 1888 to 1892, therefore, Thérèse practised humility assiduously and tried by all means possible to pass unnoticed by her sisters. She wished to be seen by Jesus alone, to give him more love, and to make sure that this love was absolutely pure. In 1893 and 1894 she advanced to the point of discovering her authentic spiritual poverty, surrendered herself increasingly to God's action in her soul, and waited for him to repair the powerlessness of her love with the strength and munificence of his love for her.

The word 'abandonment' appears for the first time in her writings in a letter to Céline dated 6 July 1893. Thérèse was certainly well acquainted with the concept, for her sisters had explicitly encouraged her to practice 'abandonment' when she was experiencing such difficulties about entering Carmel:

> I spent the afternoon of the radiant feast [Christmas] in tears, and I went to see the Carmelites. My surprise was indeed great when they opened the grille, and there I saw a radiant little Jesus holding a ball in his hand and on it was written my name. The Carmelites, taking the place of Jesus who was too little to speak, sang a hymn to me which was composed by my dear Mother; each word poured consolation into my soul. Never shall I forget this delicate attention of a maternal heart that always covered me with exquisite tenderness. After thanking all by shedding copious tears, I told them about the surprise Céline gave me when I returned from Midnight Mass. I found in my room, in the center of a charming basin, a little boat carrying the Little Jesus asleep with a little ball at his side, and Céline had written these words on the white sail: 'I sleep but my heart watches,' and on the boat itself this one word: 'Abandonment!' Ah! though Jesus was not yet speaking to his little fiancée, and though his divine eyes remained closed, he at least revealed himself to her through souls who understood all the delicacies and the love of his Heart. (A 67 v–68 r; Au 142–3)

But previously she had not adopted the word itself into her vocabulary. It was not a feature of her mental and intellectual environment, or of her spiritual agenda. When it became a familiar aspect of her psychology the differences were considerable. For example, in 1887 her abandonment issued from a 'trial' and was accompanied by 'grief', but in 1897 it was the outcome of a positive perception of God as the One who drew her mercifully to himself, filling her with profound joy. In 1887 her abandonment was limited to the practical difficulties she had to overcome, whereas it is not excessive to say that in later years it became an all-encompassing way of life. This 'new' form of abandonment, designated specifically as such (and apparently used thus for the first time in her 1893 letter to Céline), was very different from the abandonment of six years earlier and much closer to the final reality of her spiritual life.

Thérèse describes her new perceptions as follows in her letter to Céline:

> Merit does not consist in doing or in giving much, but rather in receiving, in loving much. ... It is said it is much sweeter to give than to receive, and it is true. But when Jesus wills to take for himself the sweetness of giving, it would not be gracious to refuse. Let us allow him to take and give all he wills. Perfection consists in doing his will. (LT 142; LC 153).

This represents a considerable change from the viewpoint of 1889, when sanctity 'had to be achieved at the point of a sword' by the sole salutary method of 'suffering from everything'. Thérèse's ideal still consisted in 'loving much', but her personal effort was now marked by abandonment to God's will, whatever form it took, even if it contradicted her former course of 'suffering much'. Now she cared very little for her love and its standing in God's eyes: '... how easy it is to please Jesus, to delight his Heart, one has only to love him, without looking at one's self, without examining one's faults too much' (*ibid.*).

The letter continues in the same vein, yet it probes even more deeply. Thérèse has scarcely become indifferent to her failings, but Jesus teaches her simply: 'to draw profit from everything, *from the good and the bad* she finds in herself' (*ibid.*).

Jesus has taught her a new 'plan of salvation':

> He is teaching her to play at the bank of love, or rather he plays for her and does not tell her how he goes about it, for that is his affair and not Thérèse's. What she must do is abandon herself, surrender herself,

without keeping anything, not even the joy of knowing how much the bank is returning to her. (*ibid.*)

Thérèse never recommended a nonchalant attitude to the love of God. She never proffered easy solutions or what Bonhoeffer called 'cheap grace'. But she did begin to expect much more from God himself, and did so explicitly. In fact this enabled her to look at her weaknesses with growing compassion. She now saw everything in due perspective and could be more at ease with her helplessness. She did everything she could do, and recognized that the Lord was good and powerful enough to supplement any failures, so that his strength made up for the inadequacy of her fragility. Thérèse maintained this attitude from now on.

The same letter shows a familiar notion growing in clarity and intensity:

… my director, who is Jesus, teaches me not to count up my acts [as when she was preparing for her First Communion]. He teaches me to do *all* through love, to refuse Him nothing, to be content when he gives me a chance of proving to him that I love him. But [here we perceive her major new conviction] all this is done in peace, in *abandonment,* it is Jesus who is doing all in me, and I am doing nothing. (*ibid.*)

It is almost as if this daughter of two careful business persons had surrendered her account books to a superior and more competent auditor.

'Jesus is doing all in me, and I am doing nothing.' This is a succinct description, in Thérèse's own words, of her new perspective in the search for holiness. Her own will capitulates in this respect as elsewhere. With due simplicity and a certain degree of humour, she acknowledges her powerlessness and ranks her personal efforts appropriately. As she wrote to Céline shortly after that:

Perhaps you will think that I always do what I am saying. Oh, no! I am not always faithful, but I never get discouraged. I abandon myself into the arms of Jesus. The little drop of dew goes deeper into the calyx of the flower of the fields [Jesus], and there it finds again all it has lost and even much more. (LT 143; LC 154)

All wish to perform well and desire to accumulate good spiritual marks have disappeared: 'It is not for the purpose of weaving my crown, gaining merits, it is in order to please Jesus ...' (*ibid.*).

A Step Away from Spiritual Childhood

But surely all the foregoing represents a satisfactory account of the famous 'little way' that Thérèse repeatedly refers to from now on? Can there be anything more to add to the child-and-father relationship that was now to become an essential component of Thérèse's spirituality?

We have observed her life-long insistence on fidelity in 'small matters'. Yet, from 1893 onward, she considered merit and progress to be no longer her concern but God's. Thérèse had a keen awareness of her own inadequacies and therefore was interested not so much in transforming her weakness into love as in allowing the Lord himself to work in her. She was already convinced of the precedence of God's love, which is not only the basis but the perfection of our acts of love, and consequently she might be thought to have been practicing her 'little way' fully even at this early stage.

Of course, even now she lived essentially as a child of the Father, yet she managed to integrate the above elements and attitudes into an appropriately satisfactory whole only in her final understanding of the spiritual life. In the meantime, Thérèse was still gathering the materials she needed to achieve the ultimate synthesis that we now recognize as her unique form of spirituality. We must take her seriously when we read her later claim that only at that point had she discovered a truly new way. In this phase, she had the building blocks and the design, so to speak, but the construction was not yet complete. Thérèse still had to reformulate her notion of holiness for the last time, and to decide on a final hierarchy of values. In 1893 she was not far from the definitive synthesis of her 'little way'. To change the metaphor, the bud was about to bloom.

Thérèse's own terminology in that letter to Céline in 1893 is helpful here. By then Thérèse had become aware of the divine 'strategy' in her journey towards sanctity but did not yet understand 'how he managed to make her love yield its increase'. When she eventually reached a full understanding of her 'little way', the Lord would reveal to her precisely how it was to be accomplished, and then everything would fall into place. Thérèse would be able to adapt herself to his strategy; the path would open before her; she would run along the road ahead, clearly signposted and brightly lit. Formerly she had walked along like a sightless pilgrim, subject to all the hesitations, errors and delays suffered by the blind. But now she would take wing and fly.

Thérèse herself explains that her great discovery relied on God himself. She found out that the nature of his loving-kindness was apparent in its actual exercise as mercy. Of course she had become aware of God's goodness and had seen how effective it could be. Now she would learn that God as love was not only real, pre-eminent and faithful but stooped down to his creatures. His was a love that sought out the lowly in order to fill them to the brim precisely because they were lowly. Thérèse would discover the mercy of God as the vital source of her entire life, the secret of her redemption and sanctification.

We might summarize the points made in this chapter, and the advice we have gleaned from Thérèse's life and writings so far, by saying that accepting our limitations is not a mere aspect but an essential component of openness to God. Thereafter our lowliness will not result mainly from humility but will develop from trust. In future our confident surrender to God's mercy of the helplessness we have already acknowledged will shine out as a sure sign and beacon of his loving intervention.

⤜ 3 ⤛

Empty Hands Ready for Merciful Love

THÉRÈSE LIVED THROUGH the final stages of her father's steady decline at a distance. Monsieur Martin was cared for lovingly by Léonie and Céline, but he died on 29 July 1894. Thérèse felt that he was very close to her:

> Papa's death does not give me the impression of a death but of a real *life*. I am finding him once more after an absence of six years, I feel him around *me*, looking at me and protecting me. (LT 170; LC 160)

Less than two months later Céline abandoned the everyday world for the Carmel of Lisieux. There were now four sisters from the same family in the small community. This was a new situation in the history of the Order. Thérèse had no objections to it; on the contrary, she was overjoyed at the prospect:

> Dear Céline . . . Fear nothing, Jesus will not misguide you. . . . I suffered so much for you that I hope I am not an obstacle to your vocation. Has not our affection been purified like gold in the crucible? (LT 168; LC 159)

Céline's trousseau for the novitiate included a camera, which produced the many photographs of Thérèse taken with the full assent of Sister Agnes, prioress at the time. Fortunately for us, Pauline had a very broad-minded attitude to modern technology. More importantly, Céline brought a small notebook with her that was destined to play a significant role in Thérèse's life. It contained an anthology of some of the most beautiful texts of the Old Testament. The young Carmelites of Lisieux were not allowed to read that 'strange' old book in its entirety. Therefore the Old Testament was accessible to Thérèse only through liturgical texts and other spiritual works. But now Céline's thoughtfulness had provided Thérèse, an avid reader of Scripture, with a rich selection.

An 'Entirely New Little Path'

Not long afterwards, and certainly before the end of the year, Thérèse made a brilliant discovery while meditating on the texts in Céline's notebook. She had found her famous 'little way'. We need no objective exegetical analysis of the relevant texts to understand the simple truth that Thérèse's search was divinely inspired. Her discovery relied mainly on an inward onrush of the Holy Spirit, who enabled her to 'understand' these texts 'with the heart' (Matt. 13: 15). They acted as something like the lens of a magic lantern that allowed the whole treasury of faith to be projected on the screen of Thérèse's consciousness. At such grace-filled moments Thérèse clearly perceived the lines of force running beneath the surface of all Revelation. She also experienced the undercurrents of divine life in her own existence. Through authentic 'spiritual' readings God communicated personal messages to her that would last the rest of her life.

Only a few months before her death she related the story of her 'Eureka' ('I have found it!') occasion. Her account shows how her thinking had developed from the point when she discovered her 'way'. Two and a half years had elapsed since then. The passage (C 2 v–3 r) is too long to be reproduced here in full. Nevertheless, I can summarize five salient points:

(1) Thérèse mentions an old desire with which we are already familiar: 'I have always wanted to be a saint.' From the outset, the new 'little way' – this is Thérèse's own expression – revealed its pragmatic character. It was not an end in itself but an intermediate period, a link, a passage, and a bridge leading to the goal, which was holiness or love in full maturity.

(2) But who can produce such a love? Thérèse knew that she could not do so alone. This well-established longing was

accompanied by an equally venerable conviction of her helplessness:

> I always wanted to be a saint, but alas! I've always noticed, whenever I compared myself with the saints, that between them and me there is the same difference that exists between a mountain whose summit is lost in the clouds and an obscure grain of sand.

We have witnessed her lifelong struggle between desire and helplessness, much like the desperate combat between Jacob and Yahweh (Gen. 32). Of course we can argue on the basis of objective facts and try to relativize the holiness of this saint among others by emphasizing Thérèse's humble opinion of herself. But what is important is Thérèse's personal feelings on the matter. They constitute the point of departure of her 'little way' (God gives his light to the humble). A vital question is involved here, and a construct that seems to reflect the experience of many believers, albeit on a smaller scale. The answer of the saint of Lisieux easily finds a universal echo in the Church.

(3) Thérèse's is the vital response of someone who has lived in the light of divine revelation for a long time, and who now sees with increasing acuity how God is leading her. An intimate personal assurance forbids her to surrender to confusion and discouragement:

> Instead of discouraging myself, I said to myself: God would not inspire impractical desires, therefore I may aspire to holiness despite my littleness.

It is highly improbable that when she made her discovery Thérèse actually reasoned just like that, in so many words. Undoubtedly she experienced a sudden liberating intuition which, like a seed, fell into fertile soil well prepared to nourish it. This conviction was already fully alive and had become a constant for her. She would never make it on her own, yet her heart would not let her give in. In her own words:

> To grow is impossible for me; I must endure myself such as I am with

all my imperfections. But I do want to look for the means of going to heaven [in fact, Thérèse meant climbing to the summit of holiness] by a little path that is very straight and very short: an entirely new little path.

(4) Aware of her littleness, which had attempted so much, and convinced of the powerlessness of her love, Thérèse approached the Scriptures, and therefore God himself, in quest of a solution. Her abandonment of 1893 was neither profound nor luminous enough to satisfy her completely. Moreover, things were not working out fast enough, or with sufficient certainty. Now Thérèse looked for a spiritual elevator that would carry her to the highest level of sanctity. The metaphor of an elevator in her imagery was wholly original. It originated in her youthful journey to Rome in 1888, when she saw elevators in hotels for the first time. She had found them fascinating. Nowadays she would probably talk of escalators and ski lifts, or even of space rockets. In any case, compared with an elevator that took one effortlessly to the top, stairs were very tiring. As for steps of the spiritual variety, Thérèse found them not only tiring but fruitless as well.

(5) At long last Thérèse happened on the truly liberating answer. It came from a quotation from Proverbs 9: 4 that she found in her anthology: 'Whoever is very little, let him come to me.' Very little. Thérèse was moved by these words but also felt personally challenged by them. For a long time now, the tiny grain of sand had been aspiring to littleness, but by way of humility. Littleness in holiness was the problem she had been wrestling with for some time. But now, in her littleness, she could approach God. He had something to tell her about himself and about her ascent to the summit of holiness. Trusting entirely in the Lord, Thérèse turned to him with a heart full of hope and completely receptive. She continued her search for further messages. Not surprisingly, a few pages later she came upon Isaiah 66: 12–13. Speaking for Yahweh, the text said: 'As a mother caresses her child, so shall I comfort you; I will carry you on my breast and rock you on my knees.' This was a precious find for Thérèse and sparkled as attractively as any diamond!

I have quoted the texts almost as Thérèse found them in her

anthology. But in the Revised Standard Version, for example, the text is rendered thus: 'Whoever is simple let him turn in here', and the Ecumenical Translation says: 'Is there a simple-hearted man? Let him come here!' The French expression '*tout petit*' ('very little', Vulgate '*parvulus*'), does not appear in similar versions. Thérèse would probably never have responded to the illumination she found in her anthology if she had consulted such standard translations. God often comes to us in chance encounters; his workings are indeed mysterious to behold. If she had consulted a different version, Thérèse might not have made her discovery, or she might have found it elsewhere, or even discovered at a later date what she had now come to understand. Sooner or later God would have revealed the same message, to be sure, but now the time was exceptionally ripe for it.

The light that shone from Isaiah's text was indeed dazzling. 'Ah, never have words more tender, more melodious, rejoiced my soul. Your arms are the elevator which must lift me up to Heaven, O Jesus!'

And here is another expression replete with symbolism: the arms of Jesus. With these words Thérèse states that God, not human beings, will lead her to holiness. But on what condition? 'For this I don't need to grow up; on the contrary I must remain *little* and become ever more so', until indeed she becomes '*absolutely*' little! Then, and only then, God *will grant* her everything 'as a mother [grants something to] her infant child!'

At last Thérèse has understood the one needful thing. She has finally arrived at the idea that her fundamental task is one of being receptive, and completely, widely open to the saving, caring and nurturing love of God's maternal heart. Thérèse must no longer try to save herself. Instead she must accept being saved and sanctified, and for that she must surrender herself with absolute trust in the God who offers her his gratuitous, overflowing love. Hence this song of praise from her heart: 'O my God, you have exceeded my expectations, and I wish to celebrate your tender mercies!'

Let us look more closely at the meaning of this. God is depicted here as very attentive to us, his creatures; and as inviting us to open ourselves up, just as we are, to his strong and gratuitous tenderness. If our faith and gratitude lead us to surrender and draw near to the living God, the Lord will surely touch us with his creative and unifying love, which will make us more precious and lovable, and more like God himself. The grace of the Spirit – the 'living water' (John 4: 10–14) which refreshes and enlivens – will penetrate our whole being. 'I will carry you' – as a mother, the child of her love! The reality of divine 'mercy' is seen to radiate outwards in the course of this description; that is, the reality of God's indwelling in a heart because of its 'misery', of a God stooping to care for his lowly creature, is felt and appreciated.

As mature adults we must have the courage to appear before God in all our spiritual poverty without being fatalistic or fearful, but with entire confidence. To be numbered among those who are called, or, better (for all *are* called), to be receptive to God's liberal self-bestowal, we will acknowledge our 'absolute littleness' in that humility born of recognizing what we are in truth and yet how much we are loved by God. Moreover, to take this line of reasoning further, we will have to 'come' to him in blind abandonment, knowing that, paradoxically, blindness in this case is sight at its keenest.

This is the core of what Thérèse grasped intuitively when she found her 'little way'. She called it 'entirely new' because, after a long and painful walk through brushwood and forest, a clear, straight pathway opened up for her that she did not hesitate to take without fear of going astray. If she proclaimed it 'entirely new', it was also because, spanning the era of Jansenism as it did, this 'little way' was directly connected with Jesus, who had said: 'The Spirit of the Lord is upon me, because he anointed me to preach good tidings to the poor: he hath sent me to proclaim release to the captives, and recovering of sight to the blind, to set at liberty them that are bruised, to proclaim the acceptable year of the Lord' (Luke 4: 18–19).

When she made this discovery, Thérèse's intuition was still in an early stage of development. In the months ahead she would need to assimilate her liberating new ideas fully, to learn to put her absolute trust into everyday practice, and to formulate her prophetic message for those who would come after her.

For the present, her life was wonderfully transformed! All concern over herself had vanished. Her quest for sanctity was basically free of restraints. God himself was stooping down to her; God himself was coming to meet her. In future, the road would be clear and wide open.

There was a song in Thérèse's heart too: Jesus will bring my life to the point of completion, and will make me a saint. I shall do my best. I shall do what I can, but I won' t be the one who will actually be doing it, for the Lord will be the one to work in mysterious ways, in me and through me. If I should fail, he will put things right: in this life perhaps, gradually or in a powerful demonstration of his grace such as that granted me once at Christmas; or only at that blessed moment of our final meeting in heaven, where I expect to go and live life in its ultimate fullness.

Thérèse knew with total certainty that this was her path, and the last path she would follow. If she journeyed along it to its logical conclusion, it would end where God wanted to see it end: in, that is, that full participation in his own life of love which he had designed for her and for each soul individually. God would grant her the love that she could not attain by herself, and he would endow it with the language and signs peculiar to love, especially the sign of trust.

The Bible tells us that one day children were brought to Jesus for his blessing. The disciples were visibly annoyed. Did children really matter to that degree? Surely the Master had more important tasks to be concerned about? They brushed them off, roughly. Whereupon Jesus grew indignant and said: 'You must let little children come to me: never stop them. For the kingdom of God belongs to such as these. Indeed, I assure you that the man who does not accept the kingdom of God like a little child will never enter it' (Mark 10: 13–15). Thérèse bore this in mind and resolved to 'remain' little, and to 'welcome' and receive the kingdom from the Lord's own hands, purely and simply.

We have seen how Thérèse summed up her future plan of action in her determination to be 'very little', an expression she had borrowed from Proverbs 9: 4. In the few years that were left of her life, she often called herself 'the very little one' (*la toute petite*). It was her ideal, motto, watchword, call sign and theme song, and she liked to underline the two words – following her custom of emphasizing favorite quotations or her own words meant strongly. In this instance she referred to the original text from Scripture that had prompted her new spiritual under-standing. The entire dynamics of trust in the faithful mercy of God was contained in these two words.

'Mercy' was another word that she used in a specific way from the time of her great discovery. Certainly Thérèse was well acquainted with the concept from her spiritual reading and from chanting the psalms in choir. But the word started to resonate in her heart only from the end of 1894. The bulk of her writings before 1895 (some 350 pages of letters, poems and plays) feature the noun 'mercy' only once, and the adjective 'merciful' also appears only once. However, after her discovery, the first part of her autobiography alone (i.e. the A manuscript, amounting to some 200 printed pages) uses the word 'merciful' over twenty times, demonstrating the truth of the adage: 'Of the fullness of the heart the lips will speak.'

When young Sister Thérèse of the Child Jesus settled down to write the prologue to her autobiography by the light of her kerosene lamp on that bitterly cold evening in January 1895, she was bound to utter a heartfelt song of praise to that mercy she now discerned more clearly than ever before running like a golden thread through the fabric of her story. She would hold on to that thread of mercy from which her future, so full of promise, was suspended for the last thirty-two months of her life.

A Brief Theology of Divine Mercy

The year 1895 was marvelous for the young Carmelite. It was the happiest, sunniest year of her entire life. She was now twenty-two and had been a member of the community for seven years. She felt totally at home. Admittedly, the religious life was demanding and her health was not good – she sometimes suffered from minor throat ailments – but she had never seen her vocation in such clear and simple terms and its prospects so fruitful. In February she wrote a long poem developing these impressions. Here are two of the fifteen stanzas:

Living on Love

Living on Love is giving without limit
Without claiming any wages here below.
Ah! I give without counting, truly sure
That when one loves, one does not keep count!
Overflowing with tenderness, I have given everything,
To His Divine Heart. Lightly I run.
I have nothing left but my only wealth:
Living on Love.

Living on Love is keeping within oneself
A great treasure in an earthen vase.
My Beloved, my weakness is extreme.
Ah, I' m far from being an angel from heaven!
But if I fall with each passing hour,
You come to my aid, lifting me up.
At each moment you give me your grace:
Living on Love.

(PN 17; p. 90)

In community Thérèse fared well. Her talents were acknowledged and called upon whenever necessary. For example, she could paint and she could write verses. Indeed, she became the community poet, after a fashion. If a jubilee, a ceremony of vesture or a profession was being planned, Thérèse was ready to enhance the celebrations with her poems. For the prioress's feast or that of the lay Sisters, or again for the Christmas recreations, Sister Thérèse was asked to compose something like a little play. In slightly over four years she wrote eight of these dramatic pieces (two of which were major products and based on the life of Joan of Arc, her girlhood ideal) and fifty-four poems. She also kept up a running correspondence of sorts, and now was in the process of writing the 'memoirs of her youth' at the request of her sister, Pauline, who was prioress at the time.

In addition to the demands on her sister's writing talents, two years before this Pauline had asked her (1893) to act as assistant novice mistress to Mother Marie de Gonzague. In Thérèse's own words, she became 'the little hunting dog' of the shepherdess. True, at the beginning her task was not too strenuous. Sister Martha was the only novice. She was not very intelligent perhaps, but at least she was well-disposed towards Thérèse. But six months later Sister Mary Magdalen, a postulant lay Sister, entered Carmel. She had been asked by Sister Agnes to talk to Sister Thérèse every Sunday for half an hour. But the tight-lipped peasant girl did everything to thwart any effort at communication on the part of Thérèse.

In the meantime, Thérèse, by then professed for three years, should have left the novitiate to join the community group, even though she would have had no voice in government of the community because of the presence of her two elder sisters. However, she herself had asked to stay behind and was allowed to do so because she was so young. She remained there until her death in 1897.

From the summer of 1894, Thérèse's responsibilities increased. First, in June a vivacious young girl from Paris entered and became a favourite of Thérèse's. Of all her novices, this one, known as Sister Marie de la Trinité, was at the time the only one younger than Thérèse. Next came her own sister Céline, who entered three months later and raised the number of Martin sisters to four. Last of all to enter under Thérèse was their cousin, Marie Guérin. This brought the total number of novices up to five, a good number for so young a novice mistress. But that did not deter Sister Agnes from asking Thérèse whether she would also consider praying and sacrificing herself in a very special way for a young seminarian by the name of Maurice Bellière. Thérèse's joy was complete: a future 'brother-priest'. Thérèse, who had never known her own brothers, both dead in infancy, was in seventh heaven. She wrote:

> Mother, it would be impossible for me to express my happiness . . . not
> for years had I experienced this kind of happiness. I felt my soul was
> renewed; it was as if someone had struck for the first time musical
> strings left forgotten until then. (C 32 r; Au 251)

By the light of her recently found 'entirely new little path', Thérèse saw everything swimming in an ocean of divine mercy. When, at the beginning of 1895, she became involved in writing her youthful memoirs, she clearly stressed the 'mercies of the Lord!' (A 2 r).

In itself, the prologue to her autobiography is a profound meditation. Thérèse considers her life as the object of a great 'mystery'. But that mystery was not impenetrable. It had become transparent and familiar, as, indeed, it could be to anyone, even if he or she was not entitled to it. It was a question not of 'being worthy' but of being the object of Someone's good pleasure. Thérèse called on St Paul (Rom. 9: 15–16): 'I will have mercy on whom I have mercy, and I will have compassion on whom I have compassion. It is obviously not a question of human will or human effort, but of divine mercy.'

Why was there this 'mystery' in God? Why did some people apparently benefit from it more than others? Why, Thérèse wondered, was this abundant mercy available to Paul, Augustine – and she could have included herself though it did not occur to her for a second – whereas others never received any 'extraordinary favors'? Why were there these 'preferences' in the heart of God?

'For a long time' the problem of predestination had troubled Thérèse's soul. Now she received a certain amount of illumination that almost completely resolved her doubts. The Lord was instructing her through 'Nature's own book'. Thérèse delighted in these lessons. One day she wrote to Céline:

> ... if in the order of nature Jesus is pleased to sow beneath our feet marvels so delightful, it is only to aid us into reading into more hidden mysteries of a superior order that he is working at times in souls. (LT 134; LC 148)

Once again Nature had revealed something of the profound designs of God. Thérèse was discovering in the enormous variety of flowers an illustration of God's plan for the salvation of souls. Each one, great or small, glorifies the Lord in his or her own way. The small are not, for all that, less perfect. Provided they mature as intended, they are perfect in the eyes of God, just as every flower in full bloom is beautiful. What, indeed, is perfect in his eyes? Thérèse offers us a masterly definition: 'Perfection' consists 'in *being* what he wants us to be' – and eventually in *becoming*, with the help of his mercy, what he wants us to become. It could not be better expressed. Seen thus, holiness is no longer a problem.

However, there is a second explanation, which is more profound and more Thérèsian: 'I understood that the love of our Lord can be revealed in the simplest soul who [and here is the condition] does not resist his grace in anything, as well as in the sublimest of souls' (LT 134; LC 148).

The lowly are called to radiate God's goodness even more brightly, for it is their specific mission. The workings of grace can be as fruitful in the lowliest as in the most favoured of beings, on condition that the former continue to turn to God. Without these poorest of poor souls God could not reveal himself sufficiently, for 'it seems that God would not stoop low enough', whereas, by lowering himself completely, as to a child or to a primitive creature, says Thérèse, '*God reveals his infinite grandeur*'. It is not our poverty that blocks his mercy:

> Just as the sun shines simultaneously on the tall cedars and on each little flower as though it were alone on the earth, so our Lord is occupied particularly with each soul as though there were no others like it; and just as in nature all the seasons are arranged in such a way as to make the humblest daisy bloom on a set day, in the same way everything works out for the good of each soul. (A 3 r; Au 14–15).

Then Thérèse reverts to her personal history. When writing her autobiography, what else could she do but relate the 'kindnesses' of the Lord, the 'altogether gratuitous attentiveness of Jesus'? She had no intention of including her own contribution for, ever since she began playing at 'banking with love', her accounts have no longer balanced. She admits that there was nothing in her capable of attracting his divine attention, and that his mercy alone had accomplished everything that was good in her.

In her new attitude towards love, Thérèse affirms that the 'sign of true love is the willingness to stoop down' to the beloved. This concept does not hold true for every love or friendship. For example, in one's affection for a friend, there is no self-abasement; on the contrary, the two relate to each other on the same level, and admiration prompts one to look up to the other. An attitude of condescension would hinder, even paralyse, the friendship between them. So too the love of friendship that binds the three divine Persons in the unity that is God, is without the least self-abasement. But when God loves a human being – and this is what Thérèse has in mind – it is essentially a love between unequals, in which the Loftiest reaches out to the lowliest. It is God who, in love, calls a soul to existence, accompanies it with love, and makes reciprocity in love possible by revealing himself, not as an inaccessible Being but as a Father who engenders life and as a Brother who saves.

In God's Embrace

'All is grace' (DE 57), Thérèse said, following St Paul. But there are many circumstances in which we do not immediately recognize the far-reaching effects of grace. It is more in hindsight and with the light of the Spirit that we see how God has accompanied us with his love in painful and even ordinary situations. Then God's grace appears as an undercoat of pain which, after a long period of time, shows through the upper layers as they gradually wear out. This can account for our frequent inability to understand our past in a clear-cut fashion. By reflecting so faithfully on her own past, Thérèse gradually realized how her whole life had been guided by God. 'God's liberal mercy', she wrote: 'Therein lies the mystery of my vocation, of my entire life, and especially the mystery of the privileges of Jesus in my soul' (A 2 r).

Thérèse could have turned away from God, lost her way, perhaps even abandoned the road where God wanted her. Of a trip to Alençon as a girl she had once said:

> I was entertained, coddled and admired. ... I must admit this type of life had its charms for me. ... At the age of ten the heart allows itself to be easily dazzled, and I consider it a great grace not to have remained at Alençon. The friends we had there were too worldly; they knew too well how to ally the joys of this earth to the service of God. (A 32 v; Au 73)

With her intense love for Jesus in mind, she later added more precisely: 'With a heart like mine, I would have let myself be caught and my wings cut off' (A 38 r). Now she recognizes with gratitude that her heart had been 'raised up to God right from its awakening' (A 40 r).

That same heart was presently turned to God in its life of prayer, in a life offered to God's pure honour and love, a life called to direct and to live in that unique love all other love of persons and things.

Reflecting upon all this, Thérèse meditated on the life of St Mary Magdalen. In the depths of her heart she feels very close to her: 'With a nature like mine I would have become quite wicked, and perhaps would have lost my soul' (A 8 v):

> I have no merit at all, then, in not having given myself up to the love of creatures. I was preserved from it only through God's mercy! I know that without him, I could have fallen as low as St Mary Magdalene, and the profound words of our Lord to Simon resound with a great sweetness in my soul. I know that 'he to whom less is forgiven LOVES less' (Luke 7: 47), but I also know that *Jesus has forgiven me more* than St Mary Magdalene since he forgave me in advance by preventing me from falling. (A 38 v; Au 83)

Thérèse was convinced that one loves more when removing stumbling-blocks than when helping someone else to rise after a fall. That was what God had done for her when he removed the snares and stones over which she could have stumbled. Consequently she knew she was loved more intensely by the Lord, who did not come for those who were sure of their own virtue but for sinners like herself (Matt. 9: 13). Her conclusion was that:

> He wants me to love him because he has forgiven me, not much, but ALL. He has not expected me to love him much like Mary Magdalene, but he has willed that I KNOW how he has loved me with a love of unspeakable *foresight* in order that now I may love him unto *folly!* I have heard it said that one cannot meet a pure soul who loves more than a repentant soul; ah! how I would wish to give the lie to this statement! (A 39 r; Au 84)

An intuitive knowledge of the divine mercy that shoulders everything had led her to unmask a popular fallacy. The purity of her heart had made her poor and humble, well aware of having received everything.

Thérèse continued to write her memoirs regularly, reflecting on them at great length and most fruitfully. Her recent discovery of God's maternal love and the constant awareness of his action in her soul over the years reawakened in her a new enthusiasm and a spirit of fervent gratitude. One day, when examining her life's experiences as usual, she 'heard' God speak to her.

It was on 9 June 1895, to be exact – a bright, radiant spring morning and the feast of the Holy Trinity – that a marvellous meeting with the Lord took place in Thérèse's heart during the Eucharist. She suddenly received 'the grace to understand better than ever how much Jesus desires to be loved' (A 84 r).

'How much Jesus desires *to be loved.*' That is how Thérèse expressed herself. But the use of the passive voice, 'to be loved', means that we allow Jesus to love us actively. As for us, 'to love' means that we agree to let him love us. Jesus is loved when he is free to love us fully and when we allow ourselves to be fully loved by him.

She elaborates on her insight:

> I was thinking about the souls who offer themselves as victims of God's justice in order to turn away the punishments reserved to sinners, drawing them upon themselves. (A 84 r; Au 180)

Her intuition was guiding her reasoning. God's severe justice was still a major factor during this era tinged with Jansenism. A book on Carmelite spirituality, dubiously entitled *The Treasure of Carmel*, recommended the offering of oneself to God's Justice, and even declared this offering as one of the goals of the Order. (Commentators have said, and with reason, that certain passages of this book were terrifyingly rigoristic.) The Carmel of Lisieux included Sisters known to have made this generous, if misguided, oblation. Thérèse, too, on that morning in June had suddenly felt impelled to give herself to God more intensely and was contemplating just such an offering, even though she felt no inclination to do so. How could she, little creature that she was, take such a crushing burden of suffering on her frail shoulders?

Fortunately, the light that dazzled her on that auspicious morning was kindly too. Everything was basking in that sun of Divine Mercy which, for several months now, she had watched rising higher in her firmament. With a heart all on fire she prayed:

> O my God, will your justice alone draw souls to you as victims? Does not your merciful *Love* need victims as well? ... On all sides it is misunderstood, rejected; those hearts on whom you would bestow your love, turn to creatures, begging for happiness from their pitiable affections, instead of casting themselves into your arms and accepting your infinite *Love*. O my God, will your rejected love remain in your heart? It seems to me that if you could find souls willing to offer themselves as victims of holocaust to your Love, you would consume them rapidly; it seems to me that you would be happy to release the floods of infinite tenderness that are contained in you. O my Jesus, let *me* be that happy victim, consume your holocaust in the fire of your Divine Love! (A 83 r; Au 180–1)

And so Thérèse offered herself up.

After the celebration of the Eucharist, she lost no time in drawing up an 'act of offering', thereby revealing just how seriously she meant it. It was to be a definitive donation, and would mark a solemn and privileged moment in her spiritual journey.

The similarity between her 'little way of childhood' and this 'offering of herself' is striking. In fact, to claim that 'spiritual childhood' is one thing and the 'offering to merciful love' is another would be erroneous. From now on an intimate bond would pervade Thérèse's life and everything would gravitate around the same axis with the 'offering' completely integrated into the guidelines of the 'little way'.

This 'act' began as follows:

> O my God! Beloved Trinity, I wish to love you and to make you loved. I desire to accomplish your will in every way. In a word, I want to be

holy, but I feel my powerlessness and ask you, O my God, to be yourself my holiness. (Au 276)

The goal (holiness), the fact (her powerlessness), and the solution (God's own sanctifying action) are not new in Thérèse's life. These realities were actually very central ever since the crucial moment when Thérèse discovered her 'little way' six months before. She goes on to speak of the basis for the confident request she addresses to God, which is nothing less than the gifts and merits of Jesus' humanity, enhanced by the love and merits of Mary, the angels and the saints. Well aware that the Father would grant everything asked for in the name of Jesus (John 16: 21), Thérèse argues – as she had in the explanation of her 'little way' – that the great aspirations of her heart had to make sense: *'I know it, O my God! The more you want to give the more you make one desire.* [She had borrowed this thought from St John of the Cross.] I feel immense desires in my heart and it is with confidence that I ask you to take possession of my soul.'

Following a digression where she mentions her love, her gratitude and her hope, Thérèse renews her first promise of living entirely dependent on God's attentive mercy to which she entrusts herself unreservedly. This renewal takes on the solemnity of a vow in a spirit of perfect spiritual poverty:

> I do not want to accumulate any merits for Heaven. I want to work solely for your love, with the one intention of pleasing you, of consoling your Sacred Heart, and of saving souls who will love you eternally. In the evening of this life, I shall appear before you with empty hands, for I am not asking you, Lord, to count my works. Every one of my good deeds has blemishes in your eyes. Therefore, I would vest myself with your *Justice* and receive from your *Love* the eternal possession of yourself. I want no other Throne, no other Crown than yourself, O my Beloved. (Au 277)

Thérèse knows that the merciful intervention of Jesus exceeds our own poor efforts so very much: 'You can prepare me to appear before you in an instant.'

There follows the offering proper, the result of having long studied God's merciful love:

In order to live in an act of perfect love, I offer myself as a victim of holocaust to your Merciful Love, imploring you to consume me unceasingly and to let overflow into my soul the floods of infinite tenderness contained in you, that thus I may become a martyr to your love, O my God. . . . May this martyrdom, after having prepared me to appear before you, allow me to die at last, and may my soul without delay leap into the eternal embrace of your Merciful Love. O my Beloved, with every beat of my heart I want to renew this offering an infinite number of times until the shadows of night, having been dispelled, I can tell you of my love face to face for all eternity. (Au 277)

In a powerful gesture of loving trust, beyond the boundaries of her poverty and of time, Thérèse has established herself in the merciful heart of the All-Holy, who wishes to fill all the empty hands that stretch out to him in hopeful expectation.

In a certain sense, the 'little way' was bound to lead to such an 'offering'. The latter is like the heart of the 'little way' expressed in the form of a prayer. In line with this offering, we can speak of progress and of growth in depth in the sense that Thérèse lives and understands her little way more intensely after having actually lived it for more than six months. Thérèse understands God's merciful love 'better than ever', and abandons herself to it more effectively until this abandonment becomes second nature.

The symbolism Thérèse uses in her 'act' (and in A 84 r–v) differs considerably from that found in the exposé of her 'little way'. In the latter, Thérèse makes use of images like the 'grain of sand', the 'summit of the mountain', 'the child', the 'elevator', and the 'arms' that carry. With the exception of the 'arms' (which do not carry here, for we throw ourselves into them), all these symbols are missing in her offering. In the former, she speaks of 'waves' that 'overflow', of 'victims' who must be 'consumed' by 'fire', and also of 'vesting' oneself in divine Justice, of a 'throne' and of a 'crown' which will be God himself. But the content and the core of her experiences are the same.

Henceforth, in Thérèse's eyes God's love is essentially merciful and his mercy essentially loving. Yet in future the term 'merciful love' does not appear often. She thought it somewhat redundant to use two words for what could be said in one. From now on, one word will suffice: love! Love, simply love, because in her eyes, when it is a question of God's love for us, it is essentially merciful. Consequently, when, at the end of the first part of her autobiography, Thérèse notes the memorable dates in her life, she lists 9 June 1895 simply as the 'offering of myself to Love'.

From a pastoral standpoint, and in the spirit of Thérèse, this offering to merciful love cannot be interpreted or used as a kind of magic formula which can be pronounced once and will then take care of everything for the rest of one's life. The trusting movement towards God must become truly vital, like the 'beat of the heart' mentioned by Thérèse. More than with words, the offering must be renewed in daily living, and demands a joyous and tireless emergence from self and a constant confident giving of oneself to God. Then we shall know his most profound Being, for God loves to be love, and love is his ecstasy, his life in the Trinity, his mystery, and the secret of his gratuitous creation, of redemption and of heaven.

Waves of Grace

With the offering of herself to Love, Thérèse had reached the summit. Truly, 1895 was the 'year' of divine mercy for her. That day of 9 June had released many repressed impulses. Now the waves of divine love that she had called for in her offering inundated her soul. It was a festive time of full life, joy, and a profusion of divine experiences. Never before had Thérèse been so overwhelmed by the tangible presence of God. The desert of a few years earlier had changed completely. 'I will open rivers on the bare heights, and fountains in the midst of the valleys; I will make the wilderness a pool of water, and the dry land springs of water' (Is. 41: 18).

Those 'streams of living water' that Jesus had promised were flowing in Thérèse's heart (John 7: 38–9). This period in Thérèse's life is clearly marked by a certain degree of mysticism. Six months after her consecration to Mercy, she recalled the recent flooding of her soul:

You know the rivers, or rather the oceans of grace that flooded my soul. ... Ah! Since the happy day, it seems to me that *Love* penetrates and surrounds me, that at each moment this *Merciful Love* renews me, purifying my soul and leaving no trace of sin within it. ... (A 84 r; Au 181)

This was indeed living out of God's hand! Her sole reaction was: 'Now I have no other desire save that of loving Jesus to death' (A 82 v). Her desires had been effectively stripped of all personal plans and personal ambition. The road to sanctity was now crystal clear:

I always feel ... the same bold confidence of becoming a great saint because I don't count on my merits since I have *none*, but I trust in him who is Virtue and Holiness. God alone, content with my weak efforts, will raise me to himself and make me a *saint*, clothing me in his infinite merits. (A 32 r; Au 72)

Now her hope had become theological, based not on herself but on the love of Jesus, who can transform deficiencies into occasions for dispensing his generous affection.

Her fondest dream was to abandon herself entirely to him:

Neither do I desire any longer suffering or death, and still I love them both; it is *love* alone that attracts me, however. ... Now, abandonment alone guides me. I have no other compass! I can no longer ask for anything with fervor except the accomplishment of God's will in my soul. (A 83 r; Au 178)

~⚜ 4 ⚜~

In the Night of Faith

THE LIGHT FLOODING into and suffusing Thérèse's soul lasted until spring 1896: 'At that time I enjoyed a faith so lively, so clear, that the mere thought of heaven made me completely happy' (C 5 v).

Nevertheless, one incident cast a shadow over her heart, even though briefly. Sister Agnes' three-year term as prioress was scheduled to expire on 21 March, and the chances of her re-election seemed excellent. However, after seven difficult rounds of the ballot, Mother Marie de Gonzague, and not Sister Agnes, carried the vote on the eighth round. Thérèse had not attended the chapter. When she heard the news, she was dumbfounded (so witnesses testified), but soon took hold of herself. Except for this disappointment, the year was pure bliss.

In the meantime Holy Week, in which each day overflows with the great mystery of divine love, had already begun. On the eve of Good Friday Thérèse vomited blood for the first time. She had a second attack the next night. But she was happy, for she imagined she could hear the distant murmuring of her Bridegroom announcing his arrival.

But the bride was not quite ready. She still needed to undergo the purifying work of additional suffering. Now the sun disappeared from her horizon and the night descended on her, plunging her into a frightful darkness. Thérèse had been happily riding her 'elevator' up to heaven when the power was suddenly cut off. She did not know where she was, how long her plight would last, or whether help would come.

Good Friday Continues

According to the autobiographical B manuscript, this dark night began 'on Easter Sunday' (B 2 r), and therefore two days after she coughed blood so copiously. But, according to the C manuscript, it had started 'during the joyful days of the Paschal season' (C 5 v). I am inclined to think that it was essentially linked with the events of Good Friday.

The mystic in Thérèse thought: 'Behold the Bridegroom, he is on his way!' But the realistic little thinker in her was soon aware that tuberculosis had attacked her lungs. In a short while her body would be let down into the earth and her soul would ascend to heaven. But what if there was no heaven? That question had already been posed, as we have seen. It was a question that came from the depths of her psyche, which, ever since her mother's premature death, had needed the security that no one can do without entirely. Like an obsession, it was about to engulf her faculties in a sea of psychic black ink and anchor itself harshly in her vigorous young mind. By the time Thérèse found herself on the point of death, leaving earth on her way to God's unknown country, heaven as a destination had lost every semblance of familiar reality. She even found it strange and distressing:

> Jesus made me feel that there were souls who had no faith. ... He permitted my soul to be invaded by the thickest darkness, and that the thought of heaven, up until then so sweet to me, be no longer anything but the cause of struggle and torment. (C 5 v; Au 211)

More than other privileged souls, Thérèse would be purified in her faith until nothing remained but the pure gold of the total gift of her self, and all because of Jesus alone: 'Now this trial is stripping me of whatever natural satisfaction I may have derived from the desire I had for heaven' (C 7 v).

Why was she still convinced that heaven was not a projection of one's deepest desires? Because of Jesus – *the fact of Jesus!* Heaven, wrote Thérèse, 'is not a story invented' by humans, but a 'definite reality' and the subject-matter of the good news proclaimed by Jesus (C 5 v).

We might be tempted to think that 'the thick fog' which hid heaven from her view also obscured any thought of Jesus' divine mission, and even of God's existence, but no. In her autobiography Thérèse described her temptations as against heaven alone. She testified unmistakably to Mother Agnes that her struggles had to do with heaven (in the sense of our ultimate destination). She felt that such temptations were peculiar to her alone and could not be explained logically. She described her situation as 'strange and incomprehensible': 'Ah, but I really believe in the Thief! Everything bears upon Heaven. How strange and incomprehensible it all is' (DE 30, 71).

But the *fact of Jesus* enabled her to remain immovable in her faith in the next world as she suffered the pains of the darkest of earthly nights. Jesus' hand was there to hold her: God's grace, her faith and the personal experience of God's goodness were the divine forces that sustained her in her darkness. She felt that 'both body and soul' vegetated in 'a black hole' (DE 173) and that sometimes 'horrible serpents would hiss in her ears' (DE 62). But Jesus remained steadfast, and so did her faith. She said of the dark thoughts that assailed her: 'I endure them necessarily, but while I am enduring them, I continue to make constant acts of faith' (DE 258).

Even if she experienced no joy, she was already living the substance of heaven in the dimension of faith:

> I do not really see what more I shall have after my death that I do not already possess in this life. I shall see God, that is true! But as for being with him, I am quite there with him already on earth. (DE 45)

All this preparation was God proceeding with his purifying work, just as St John of the Cross describes the process so inimitably in his *Dark Night of the Soul*. Did God send this purification? Or did he merely grant his grace in a period of drastic mental change? It scarcely matters which course he followed. For Thérèse it was a question of believing, of maintaining her trust, and of loving. She wanted to save souls for Jesus through her suffering. Then she would be able to say with St Paul, 'I have fought the good fight, I have kept the faith' (2 Tim. 4: 7).

A Believer More than Ever

God, of course, is a very good and skilful teacher. He granted Thérèse several months of pure overflowing joy, and the experience impressed on her the reality of his love even more effectively. The memory of the Lord's generosity would sustain her throughout her deep dark night of the soul. In the meantime Thérèse passed through a 'dark tunnel' and crossed a 'desolate land', where the darkness mocked her, crying:

> You dream of light, of a native land balmy with the sweetest of scents; you dream of the eternal possession of the Creator of all these marvels, you think you will emerge some day from the fog that envelops you! Advance, go forward, rejoice in the death that will give you, not what you are hoping for, but a night deeper yet, that of the night of nothingness. (C 5 v–7 r [conflated])

Suddenly Thérèse stops, terrified. How spontaneously all this was flowing from her pen! 'I do not want to write any further, I would be afraid of blaspheming. . . .' (*ibid.*).

Some commentators have said that God was a wall for Thérèse. Not so. Thérèse had said her *faith* was no longer a transparent 'veil' – as it had been the summer before she entered Carmel, and during the summer and winter after her Offering – but a 'wall' which rose up to the sky (C 7 v). Again we encounter her metaphorical language here. She saw *believing* as like facing a wall. That was why faith was more painful to her. But *God himself* was not a wall. If her faith gave her the impression of standing before a wall both opaque and impenetrable, God was surely to be found on either side of it! He was there in that mysterious life of heaven, just as Jesus had come to tell us and as Thérèse believed; and he was here at the very centre of her anguished and troubled existence. God was present in her world, more than ever before. He was the 'base of operations' to which Thérèse held fast for dear life. Finally, Jesus was increasingly present in her thoughts: both the Jesus of the past and the Jesus of the present moment. Thérèse grasped and held his hand outstretched to her through his word and his promise:

> At each new occasion of combat, when my enemies provoke me, I
> conduct myself bravely. . . . I run toward my Jesus. I tell him I am ready
> to shed my blood to the last drop to profess my faith in the existence of
> *heaven*. (C 7 r; Au 213)

Indeed, Thérèse carried her determination to shed her blood in
proof of her faith by using it to transcribe the Creed in her New
Testament. Her faith had never been so pure and intense:

> Jesus knows well that while unable to experience joy in my faith, I try
> at least to accomplish its works. I believe that I have made more acts of
> faith in a year than in my whole life. (*ibid.*)

She no longer experienced enjoyment or felt joy in the act of
faith. Instead the 'will to believe' and the will to act in
accordance with the word of Jesus prevailed now. In the dark
night of her faith Thérèse was not a non-believer but a great
believer.

In the midst of all this, and precisely because her faith was
totally blind, Thérèse continued to experience, on a deeper
level, the joy of a love fully given, and the joy – somehow
paradoxical – of realizing how merciful the Lord was in the
midst of all that darkness:

> Despite the trial which deprives me of *all enjoyment*, I can nevertheless
> cry out: Lord, you fill me to the brim *with joy in everything you do* . . . for
> is there a greater joy than that of suffering for love of you? – Never have
> I felt so well how sweet and merciful is the Lord. He sent me this trial
> only at the time when I had the strength to endure it. (C 7 r–v
> [conflated])

God's grace had never been so fruitful in her soul. Thérèse
grasped it and held on to the invisible hand that was leading her.
She did not seek to know anything beyond what the will of
Jesus meant and had in store for her.

At the Sinners' Table

Thérèse was convinced that the unbelievers of this world would be very surprised to appear before the Lord one day and hear him say: 'Enter into my kingdom, for others have prayed for you.' This was her fondest hope and aspiration. Even in her dark night of faith she remained unswerving in her motivation to save them. 'I tell Jesus that I am happy to be deprived of enjoying his beautiful heaven while on earth, so that he will open it to poor unbelievers for eternity' (C 7 r).

There had been a time when Thérèse experienced difficulties in understanding that such people as out-and-out atheists could exist. She believed 'that they did not speak their true mind when they denied the existence of heaven' (C 5 v).

But now she knew through personal experience how violent the assaults of reason on the word of Jesus could be. For a long time she had known that natural lethargy and egotistical interests could turn one from faith. But now she understood the role of grace in a simple act of faith, the extent to which it was necessary to remain faithful throughout the darkness of this night. In her own poverty she felt a kinship to 'souls who have no faith' and to 'sinners' – 'her brothers', as she called them – with whom she sat at 'that table filled with bitterness', ready to 'eat the bread of adversity alone', in order that 'all those who are not enlightened by the bright torch of faith might see it shine forth at last' (C 5 v–6 r [conflated]).

The original Dutch Catechism (*A New Catechism*) said of Thérèse's night of faith:

> Nothing remained of her faith except the ultimate abandonment: 'I want to believe, come to my help in the little faith that I have.' This young girl was becoming a saint worthy of occupying a place among the heroes mentioned in Hebrews 11. In the middle of the great crisis of faith that her contemporaries, the intelligentsia and the laborers of Europe, had to pass through, she endured this suffering with them in the most extreme abandonment of love for a period of eighteen months. How many lives found their birth in her surrender! (p. 346)

Like another Joan of Arc, Thérèse fought for the faith of the Church and for the triumph of good over evil. During her dark night of faith, she sympathized with the marvellous adventure of a young American who had sought refuge in a French convent. Diana Vaughan was said to be a convert who had previously dabbled to a considerable extent in demonic mysticism (something akin to what we would call Satanism). She was now intent on combating her former errors by publishing her *Memoirs*, which were creating quite a stir in French Catholic circles and even elsewhere. The Carmel of Lisieux was an ardent supporter of Diana. In her play *The Triumph of Humility*, composed for the feast of the prioress, Mother Marie de Gonzague, Thérèse had written: 'Diana Vaughan has become a new Joan of Arc. My fondest desire would be, once her mission is accomplished, to see her become united to Jesus in our little Carmel' (RP 7).

Thérèse also wrote to Diana, enclosing her own photo in the role of Joan of Arc, and, by return mail, received an answer, which she kept very carefully.

Out of fear of the Freemasons, who were said to threaten her life, Diana continued to remain in hiding, but she was so withdrawn that people grew suspicious. To put an end to all the rumours, the convert announced a press conference in Paris for 19 April 1897, which was the Monday of Easter Week. More than 400 journalists, both Catholic and anticlerical, were expected to be present and were to be shown overhead projections of her choice. Actually only one was shown, a slide photo sent, it was said, by an admirer in a community of Carmelite nuns who had depicted Diana as the 'new Joan of Arc' in a play of the admirer's own composition. The photograph in question was of Thérèse, and the very one she had sent Diana. Now, to add to the consternation of the gathering, no Diana appeared but only a certain Leo Taxtil, a Freemason and self-styled convert who, with blatant cynicism, gradually revealed to his stunned audience how for several years he had been mocking the role of Christianity in France. What about Diana? Diana had never existed! Taxtil was the sole progenitor of the entire hoax.

A few days later Thérèse received the account of the press conference and the story of her photograph. She tore 'Diana's' letter into bits and threw it on the dung heap. More than ever she realized that: 'there are truly many souls that do not have any faith, or who, through the abuse of graces, lose this precious treasure' (C 5 v).

Now she knew without a doubt for whom she was seated at the table of sinners, and for whom she was imploring the mercy of God.

Thérèse was exceptionally confident in the Lord's saving love. That is apparent once again in another play written a year earlier for her sister's feast as prioress on 21 January. Entitled *The Flight into Egypt*, this production dealt with the Holy Family seeking refuge in a grotto that served as home to a hardened felon, his wife and his little son, Dismas. The child is leprous and, without being asked, Mary cures him. But the mother, Susanna, remains anxious about his future, for he is marked by his environment and by the evil tendencies inherited from his father. Would he follow in his father's footsteps? Yes, he would do no better than his father, therefore she should harbour no illusions about him. Nevertheless, Mary predicts, gazing far into the future, her own son Jesus would tell him one day from the height of his Cross: 'Today you will be with me in Paradise.' His goodness would accompany the 'good thief' to the very end, for Jesus does not like to leave his work unfinished. As for Susanna, she must trust in God's infinite mercy and goodness, which are great enough to wash away the worst crimes when applied to the heart of a mother who places all her trust in it. 'My Jesus' does not desire the death of a sinner, but wants him or her to repent and have everlasting life (RP 6).

Thérèse retained the tendency to think and act as a 'co-redemptrix' (as it were) in her thoughts, prayer and sacrifices. This earlier play provided her with a different occasion to practise what she preached. During the performance, Sister Agnes took offence at the robbers' language, their rowdy singing, the disputes of the acting novices (prudently drinking from empty wine bottles) and, last but not least, the length of the play itself. When the performance paused for a moment, Sister Agnes seized the opportunity to bring everything to a halt. Thérèse was watching and listening from the wings, so to speak. Furtively, she dried a few tears and tried to smile as usual. But from then on, the 'dramatist' wrote much shorter plays.

✺ 5 ✺

My Vocation is Love

THÉRÈSE DID NOT FOLLOW her little way and entrust herself to God's mercy for her own sake. She had been living for two months wrapped in the bleakest darkness when Marie de Gonzague asked her to pray and to make personal sacrifices for a second 'brother-priest', Adolphe Roulland, who was about to depart for China as a missionary.

Thérèse had once formally expressed a wish to go to the Carmelite mission in Hanoi, Indo-China, so that later in the autumn of that same year her request was considered seriously, but only briefly, for it was not meant to be.

During this period her missionary ambitions were at their peak. For the sake of Jesus she must have wanted to be a missionary all over the world and from the beginning of time! Obviously these desires were impossible to fulfill. Nevertheless, they eventually blended harmoniously in her vocation to be 'the love in the heart of the Church'.

Thérèse explained all this in a long letter to her sister Marie (Sister Marie of the Sacred Heart), which became known as the B manuscript of her autobiography. This letter has stood the test of time as a priceless spiritual document. It is now acknowledged today as the 'charter' of her teaching on the concept and practice of spiritual childhood.

A Long Letter

But first, a word about the origin and the format of this letter-manuscript. In the middle of a conversation with Thérèse one day, her sister Marie had asked her to write out her 'little doctrine' (B 1 v). Without further ado, Thérèse set to work during her private (and last) retreat, beginning on 8 September, 1896, the sixth anniversary of her religious profession. First, she took two sheets of grid paper, folded them in two and proceeded to fill them completely. These eight pages form the bulk of what in time became known as MS B, or the B manuscript. Then she took another sheet of paper, and folded it too, intending to use it as a fly-leaf for the eight pages already covered in writing. However, she decided to fill in this extra sheet as well, so that what constitutes the second part in the printed version was really written first, and the first part was written second. In any case, these ten pages both summarize, and illuminate, those that were still to follow.

Meanwhile, Thérèse slipped her written work under Marie's door. Fortunately for us, the essential points of Thérèse's 'argumentation' escaped her sister's understanding. Marie could only wonder at Thérèse's impetuous desires and asked for a further explanation. The answer was not long in coming. In Letter 197, written on 17 September, Thérèse made a fresh attempt to pinpoint the essence of her 'little doctrine'. This letter now constitutes the third section of MS B. It is therefore in the foregoing order that I shall try to explain the salient points of these pages, which are certainly among the most sublime spiritual writings of all time.

The Path of Love

(1) First, Thérèse began by relating the encouraging dream she had had on 10 May 1896 (B 2 r). In her sleep she had seen the Venerable Anne of Jesus, St Teresa's right hand, who had brought the reforms of the Foundress to France and to the Netherlands. Striking up a conversation with the Venerable Anne, Thérèse asked her whether she would be going to heaven soon, and then (for the second question was as profoundly rooted in her subconscious as the first) she added: 'Tell me, is God not asking of me something more than my poor little actions and desires? Is he pleased with me?'

The answer to both questions was positive, and Thérèse woke up filled with joy. She would always think of this dream as a direct encouragement from the Lord in the middle of her bleak period of trial of faith, and also as a confirmation of the rightness of her 'way'. In fact, her little way is well summarized in these words: to do what we can with the 'poor little actions' that are in our power, and then to go on 'desiring', trusting always that the Lord will be satisfied with our feeble efforts and will give us at last what we cannot acquire ourselves. The mere telling of this dream constitutes a beautiful 'prelude' to Thérèse's 'little doctrine'.

I shall try first to analyse the expression 'poor little actions'. For Thérèse, these epithets are not charming diminutives full of air, devoid of any real meaning. Far from it. She believes in what she says, and is deeply convinced of her poverty and of her limitations. It is in that perspective that we must interpret the frequent use of the word 'little' in this manuscript. Littleness is the pure vital atmosphere in which Thérèse moves and breathes. But it conceals virtues of greater nobility. Littleness here signifies profound humility and self-forgetfulness, truth and openness to God's grace: in short, easier access for the great God in whom she places all her hope.

As for little souls, surely Jesus in his Sermon on the Mount declares the poor, simple and lowly in spirit to be blessed? Thérèse does not hesitate to side resolutely with them. She considers the lowly as the privileged class among the friends of Jesus, and fundamentally the only class he loves with spontaneity. For if we do not become as little children, who are the lowliest of all, we shall have no share in the kingdom of heaven, as he clearly says in Matt. 18: 3. Thérèse tries to avoid every semblance of pride, and that is why she likes to invoke her 'infidelities', her 'weaknesses' and her 'faults'.

It is striking how she underlined the expression 'little souls' every time she repeated it – and no fewer than seven times – in that famous Letter 197 to her sister Marie. She knows that they are 'legion' (B 5 v). She feels at home in their company, and it is for them that her 'little doctrine' is intended. In reality, of course, Thérèse describes the path that all humans must follow without exception. That this littleness in no way contradicts greatness or even magnanimity is abundantly evident from the 'immense desires' that she then explains (B 2 v–3 r). With the deepening of her love for Jesus and of her faith in God's mercy, her apostolic fervour has expanded to become universal. As a result, her impetuous aspirations will turn into a 'veritable martyrdom' for her, and the first-fruits of the martyrdom of love which she had implored in her Offering to Love earlier in June.

(2) At first, her great torment was that her numerous, even contradictory, desires apparently could not be unified or harmonized. Not a single one could be fully realized in her hidden vocation as a Carmelite. Thérèse wanted to give of herself in an unlimited fashion in a very limited lifestyle. Hers were 'hopes that bordered on the infinite' and were 'greater than the universe'; hopes that spoke of 'madness' and 'extravagances'. No one on his or her own could implement this whole range of desires that were as vast as the world itself.

Not surprisingly, an unbearable tension was produced between the dream and its practical limitations. In a very real sense, this was the sublime suffering of a great love.

(3) But then the B manuscript relates how Thérèse, on a summer's day in the same year, was meditating on 1 Cor. 12–13 and searching for an answer to her dilemma. At long last the Holy Spirit granted it to her, and with it, light and peace. She understood how love, which Paul calls the means which exceeds 'the most perfect of gifts', is the driving force of the Church. Just as the vitality of the human body depends on the beating of the heart, so the Mystical Body of Christ, which is the Church, lives on the divine love from which human hearts may draw strength and sustenance for themselves and for others. Love is the divine gift which animates the world and the sacraments of the Church, and makes its way along well-concealed paths.

I understood that it was Love alone that made the Church's members act, that if Love ever became extinct, apostles would not preach the Gospel and martyrs would not shed their blood. I understood that *Love comprised all vocations, that Love was everything, that it embraced all times and places . . . in a word, that it was eternal!* Then, in the excess of my delirious joy, I cried out: O Jesus, my Love . . . my vocation, at last I have found it, *my vocation is Love!* . . . Yes, I have found my place in the Church and it is you, O my God, who have given me this place; in the heart of the

Church, my Mother, I shall be *Love*. . . . Thus I shall be everything, and
thus my dream will be realized. (B 3 v; Au 94)

Thérèse had not ceased pursuing her first ideal of love as she
perceived it. But here it acquires its apostolic dimension. The
old ideal is now integrated in a more complete sense. Her
understanding of community will transcend all frontiers, and
her love of Jesus and his kingdom will reach a depth like the
ocean's, a vastness equal to its shores, and a fidelity lasting unto
death.

But, we are tempted to ask, wasn't Thérèse aiming too high,
well beyond her capacity? Surely she was over-extending
herself? Even though constantly driven by love, how could she
attain such an ideal when she was so little and helpless? The
answer, in MS B, is a rallying cry, renewed even more firmly,
on behalf of the 'little way' of complete confidence in God,
who will lead her to the summit of love. Thérèse's 'secret'
strategy (B 2 v) for reaching her goal consisted in remaining
radically receptive! In fact, brimming over with hope, Thérèse
did not hesitate to renew her offering to the God of mercy:

I am but a child, helpless and weak; nevertheless it is my very weakness
which gives me the boldness to offer myself as Victim to your Love, O
Jesus!

Thérèse recalls the new ways of salvation opened to us by God
through the gift of his Son: the Old Law has been succeeded by
Jesus' 'Law of Love'. The lower Love can stoop, the more it
reveals its merciful countenance:

Love has chosen me as a holocaust, weak and imperfect creature that I
am. . . . This choice, is surely worthy of Love? . . . Yes, for in order that
Love should be fully satisfied, it needs to stoop down, to stoop down to
Nothingness and to transform this Nothingness into FIRE. (B 3 v; Au
194)

Then, among other things, Thérèse explains how she would
show her generous love for Jesus and for the Church. 'Love is
proven by its works' (B 4 r), a sound principle of Thérèse's,

who was far from preaching laxism here, though she left the last word to the condescending mercy of God. Similarly, she intends to receive all her love from God himself, so that she in turn can translate it into practical evidence of love. This love, though highly radical, can assume a discreet and humble appearance as it manifests itself in the many circumstances and actions of everyday life (B 4 v–r).

In the allegory of the little bird in the next quotation, Thérèse reveals the depth of her confidence in her weakness and in her trial of faith. Her peace and joy, her resolute abandonment, and the staunchness of her faith are most impressive; but so is her refusal to give in to fear and sadness and to succumb to a feeling of desertion (B 4 v–5 r). The entire passage is written in the form of a prayer culminating in an extraordinary burst of fervor. Her thinking revolves around the dual axis of mercy and trust:

> O Jesus! Let me, in the excess of my extreme gratitude, let me tell you that your love is utter foolishness. ... How can you not expect my heart to throw itself upon you? How could my trust have any bounds? ... I am too little to do big things ... and *my particular folly* is to hope that your love will accept me as a victim. Some day, my adored Eagle, I know you will come and fetch your little bird and, carrying it off with you to the Fireside of your love, you will plunge it for all eternity into the burning abyss of that Love to which it has offered itself as victim. ... O Jesus, how I wish I could tell all *little souls* how ineffable is your condescension. ... I feel, were it not impossible, that if you found a soul weaker, lowlier than mine, it would please you to fill it with still greater favors provided it abandoned itself with complete confidence to your infinite mercy.

The pages that were written second in time but now stand as the first two of MS B shed light on the *goal* that dominated her life – 'the science of love' surpassing all riches, 'the only good that I covet' – and on the *attitude* required to receive that love:

> Jesus takes pleasure in showing me the only pathway that leads to this divine Furnace; that pathway is the *abandonment* of the small child who falls asleep without fear in the arms of its father.

To support her thesis, Thérèse called upon the two texts from Scripture that had formed the basis for her discovery of the little way (B 1 r).

Her letter to Marie (LT 197) was a fresh attempt to clarify her ideas. Thérèse argued that her ardent desires for martyrdom 'were nothing', and had nothing to do with her boundless trust. They could even be 'spiritual riches that could render one unworthy' if one took pleasure in them:

> I really feel that it is not this at all that pleases God in my little soul; what pleases him is *that he sees me loving my littleness and my poverty, the blind hope that I have in his mercy.* .... That is my only treasure. .... (LT 197; LC 170)

Not fully satisfied with these words, she explained herself even more forcefully:

> Understand that to love Jesus, to be his *victim of love*, the weaker one is, without desires or virtues, the more suited one is for the workings of this consuming and transforming Love. ... The *desire* alone to be a victim suffices, but we must consent to remain always poor and without strength, and this is the difficulty. .... (*ibid.*)

In a supreme effort to condense her thoughts, Thérèse arrived at the following formula, prodigiously simple in conception and utterance: 'It is trust, and only trust, that must lead us to love.'

As a novice Thérèse had mentioned this road to love in a letter to her cousin, Marie Guérin. The formula was very different then: 'For me, I know of no other means for arriving at perfection than love' (LT 109).

At that time Thérèse was burning with an enthusiasm that had not yet been sufficiently tested by life. She firmly believed she would succeed in fulfilling her dream of love through her own personal efforts at generosity. In spite of these efforts, six years of powerlessness and a surplus of divine inspirations had to pass before she realized that Divine Mercy was the sole cause and effect of any success she might have in achieving her dream. No doubt her experience reflects that of every serious Christian who has set himself or herself a similar goal.

Communicating the Message

During the last year and a half of her life, Thérèse spent much time formulating her doctrine with a view to transmitting it in highly condensed yet simple terms. As a result, her letters contain all kinds of concise definitions and descriptions, which she used to develop her thoughts on holiness. Her views form a coherent whole; indeed, they comprise a little 'doctrine' with its own personal stamp: 'my way', she says, 'my manner'. Thérèse was well aware that what she had produced was something out of the ordinary, and that it differed from the prevailing spirituality of her day.

Beginning with Scripture, Thérèse completed the image of God the Father by drawing spontaneously from her own personal experience of the loving and understanding figure of her own father, Louis Martin. As for the image of the *child* that she sketched, that was largely derived from her own upbringing as a little girl.

Nevertheless, this emphasis of Thérèse's on the Fatherhood of God must not lead us to infer that her piety was far from *christocentric*. On the contrary, Christ remained her centre: he was her 'spouse', but a spouse with very paternal attributes. Thérèse certainly remained the 'spouse', but a spouse who became increasingly childlike over the years.

Many factors contributed to the clear formulation of her doctrine. In the first place, there is her night of spiritual and (soon after) physical suffering. In this pain, she had to cling to the certainties of her faith and to the intuitions of her trust in God. Moreover, she had to nourish these in prayer and integrate them more consciously into her spirituality. Her life of suffering grounded her well in the doctrine she preached.

Then there was her work as mistress of formation. Since March of 1896 she had been fully responsible for the novices – without the title, however, which Mother Marie de Gonzague had reserved for herself. It was Thérèse's duty to accompany her charges, assist them, advise them, and answer their questions and objections. For the purposes of their spiritual instruction and guidance, therefore, Thérèse willingly shared her own deepest convictions with them and was always in search of symbols, examples, illustrations and anecdotes to help her convey these to her charges appropriately. She became the first evangelist of her 'little way'.

She also had her 'disciples' beyond the walls of Carmel. For example, there was Father Roulland, the missionary, for whom she prayed and with whom she corresponded. To him she most lucidly confided her thoughts on the harmony between God's mercy and his justice: because of his justice, God had to take our frailty into account and therefore had to be merciful. Then there was her sister Léonie, who had already failed three times to become a religious. Léonie particularly needed to be encouraged and in a special way. She was a typical example of the 'little soul', weak but full of good will. There was also Maurice Bellière, the seminarian, her first 'spiritual brother'. Bellière was young, very affectionate, and even sentimental (he had never known his father), but he was plagued with guilt complexes. Thérèse had his entire confidence and could open out all her little doctrine to him. Her correspondence with him on this point provides us with a rich panorama of her thought.

Towards the end of her life, we see Thérèse developing a formidable prophetic awareness of a need to carry out a 'mission' to the world (DE 102). But it was especially in the intimate exchanges with her sisters as she lay on her sick-bed that she expressed herself openly in that respect.

❧ 6 ❧

The Dynamics of Hope

IN THIS CHAPTER, after examining the way in which Thérèse's trust in God developed, I shall try to explain how her insights and experiences were combined in her visionary conception of things.

Two forces were at work in Thérèse's development. First, her own inability to produce perfect love turned her away from herself towards God, 'for whom nothing is impossible' (Luke 1: 37). Although the point of departure seems negative, the final result was positive.

The second force, which supported the first, was an inward movement that drew her to God as her new centre. She was attracted by God's mercy and taken up into his own sphere. Now the point of departure was positive and the immediate result was a greater degree of self-abnegation.

Humankind, an Incomplete Form of Being

When Thérèse felt the end approaching, she described herself increasingly as 'weak' and 'imperfect'. Should we take these judgements seriously when all contemporary testimonies unanimously praise her fidelity? Of course, we have to remember that these witnesses were only spectators. Since they were unable to penetrate into the heart's inner sanctum, the only place (if that were really possible) where purity of intention might be tested and determined, there is reason to doubt the validity of their accounts. How could they plumb the depths of a soul or judge its receptivity to grace? This inner terrain was accessible only to God and to Thérèse, for 'how true it is that God alone knows human hearts' (C 19 v; Au 234).

She also inherited faults of an earlier period, which were certainly not products of malice in any sense, but offshoots of an original plant still in need of some kind of purification. Then there was Thérèse's delicate conscience to consider, for its sensitivity had developed continually since her childhood until it registered the repercussions of every sin, even though the joyful conviction of God's mercy prevailed in the end.

Inevitably, as she grew in holiness, her sensitivity to right and wrong intensified. St John of the Cross has described vividly how, as God approaches, a feeling of unworthiness can descend on a soul and ultimately seem to envelop it. After all, the least particle of dust becomes visible in so searching and intense a beam. Ever since Thérèse had sat down with unbelievers and wrongdoers at the 'table of sinners', she had felt like one of them inwardly. One morning, during the recitation of the Confiteor, she experienced a clear conviction that she was 'a great sinner'. On the image of her crucified Lord (which had aroused so apostolic a longing in her ten years earlier), she now wrote: 'Lord, you know that I love you, but have pity on me, for I am a sinner.' Five months before her death she admitted to Abbé Maurice Bellière: 'God has not given me as a sister a *great* soul, but a *very little* and a very imperfect one' (LT 224; LC 177).

Such remarks were not intended to demonstrate her humility or to hide the truth from others. Thérèse was very serious whenever she spoke of her poverty. The inspiration for her little way came directly from her imperfect state, for her very imperfection was the soil in which her confidence took root once it had been nourished with the knowledge and conviction of God's mercy. 'Humility is truth' (CSG 19), said Thérèse, following her namesake and patron, St Teresa of Avila. It was in the light of this knowledge that she discerned the wonders of God in her own life (C 4 r), as well as the limitations that kept her from reaching her ideal state. Outwardly, there was probably no residual imperfection for which anyone might seriously have reproached her, but inwardly she scrutinized herself with the relentless eyes of a saint. We may be sure, too, that Thérèse thought of herself as still sharing the condition of those whom she advised to follow the way of trust as they tried to emerge from their imperfect state. Even if she was more advanced than most on the road, they were all pilgrims on a common route that would lead them to one and the same summit in the end.

Of course, we may find it encouraging to read how the saint of Lisieux confessed to all sorts of minor imperfections right up to the last month of her life. Examples of these peccadilloes were slight touches of impatience during her illness (LT 230) or small opportunities for self-sacrifice that she ignored (C 31 r). Although neighbourly charity had become second nature to her, she still remarked: 'I don't mean ... that I no longer have any faults; ah! I am too imperfect for that' (C 13 v; Au 222). On the other hand, the joyful realization of truth neutralized any suspicion of self-centred despondency that might have resulted from her failings:

> Jesus wants to give her nothing but his smile. ... This gentle sun, far from causing the little flower to wilt, makes her progress in a marvelous manner. She preserves, in the bottom of her calyx, the precious drops of dew she had received, and these serve to remind her always how little and weak she is. All creatures can bow toward her, admire her, and shower their praises upon her. I don't know why this is, but none of this could add one single drop of false joy to the true joy she experiences in her heart. Here she sees herself as she really is in God's eyes: a poor little thing, nothing at all. (C 2 r; Au 206)

This kind of imperfection mentioned by Thérèse is not only a given but an inescapable fact of the human condition. In her 'Offering to God's Merciful Love', Thérèse affirmed that 'all our good works are tainted in God's eyes' (Ex. 64: 5), and she predicted realistically that 'she would sometimes fall through weakness':

> It is true that no human life is exempt from faults. (LT 226; LC 178)

> ... the most holy souls will be perfect only in Heaven. (C 28 r; Au 246)

Indeed, 'a just man falls seven times [a day]' (Prov. 24: 16). Three months before her death, Thérèse made a significant admission that reveals not only a faith replete with hope in God's liberating power, but also a profound intuitive understanding of the imperfection that is bound up with all human growth in God:

> Alas! when I think of the time of my novitiate I see how imperfect I was. I made so much fuss over such little things that it makes me laugh now. Ah! how good the Lord is in having nurtured my soul, and in having given it wings. ... Later on, no doubt, the time in which I am now will appear filled with imperfections, but now I am astonished at nothing. I am not disturbed at seeing myself as weakness itself. On the contrary, it is in my weakness that I glory, and I expect each day to discover new imperfections in myself. (C 15 r; Au 224)

God is Incomparable

In yet another way, Thérèse came up against her imperfections in her deepest longings. This young woman's dream was to be able to love, and to love totally, without limit, infinitely. To that end she became poor, prayerful and vigilant, and alive with a profound sense of the Infinite. On the day of her profession she had asked for 'infinite love, without any limit other than yourself . . . love that is no longer I but you, my Jesus'. Later, in her offering to Love itself, she asked passionately for 'perfect love', the 'martyrdom of love'. The B manuscript speaks of the 'fullness of love' (B 4 v), and mentions her 'folly' of love ten times.

In loving, Thérèse discovered the potential hidden deep in the human heart. She might even be said to have become addicted to love. With every enactment of love, she heard the cry 'Again!' or 'More!' rising within her. Her capacity to love was growing steadily:

> I can see with joy that in loving him the heart expands and can give to those who are dear to it incomparably more tenderness than if it had concentrated upon one egotistical and unfruitful love. (C 22 r; Au 237)

> When the human heart gives itself to God, it loses nothing of its innate

tenderness; in fact, this tenderness grows when it becomes more pure and more divine. (C 9 r; Au 216)

And whenever love is quenched, a new thirst is produced:

> Your love is my only martyrdom.
> The more I feel it burning within me,
> The more my soul desires you ...
> Jesus, make me die
> Of Love for You!!! (PN 31; p. 151)

Throughout her entire life she longed to love the Beloved duly: that is, as he deserved to be loved; and to return as much as she had received in response to the love with which she was loved. Thérèse, the ardent lover, wanted to love God as much as he loved her. Yet, by trying to do so, she sentenced herself to inevitable even if holy failure, for God can never be loved exactly as he loves us. He will always love us first, and more profoundly, obliging our human hearts to admit that: 'God is infinitely greater than our hearts' (1 John 3: 20).

Yet love cannot but aspire to such heights. St John of the Cross says that a soul wants to love God with the purity and perfection with which he loves the soul. The soul wants to equal God's love for it, because a lover cannot be satisfied until he or she feels that he or she loves as much as he or she is loved:

This property for which the soul prays so that she may love perfectly she here calls the breathing of the air, because it is a most delicate touch and feeling which the soul feels at this time in the communication of the Holy Spirit; who, sublimely breathing with that his divine breath, raises the soul and informs her that she may breathe into God the same breath of love that the Father breathes into the Son and the Son into the Father, which is the same Holy Spirit that they breathe into her in the said transformation. For it would not be a true transformation if the soul were not united and transformed also in the Holy Spirit, albeit not in a degree revealed and manifest, by reason of the lowliness of this life. ... But the soul that is united and transformed in God breathes in God into God the same divine breath that God, being in her, breathes into her in himself ... the souls possess these same blessings by participation

> as he possesses by nature; for the which cause they are truly gods by
> participation, equals of God and his companions. (*Spiritual Canticle*, 38:
> 2–5)

Thérèse's objective was to become a channel through which God's love could flow back perfectly to him through her. But how could this channel ever be wide enough to allow infinite love to flow through it? And, if she happened to commit sins or faults, surely they would operate as so many setbacks and impairments to love ...

Almost imperceptibly, Thérèse discovered that we shall never love God *as* he loves us. He will always surpass us, and, if we try to do more, in the end we shall always be compelled to acknowledge the powerlessness of our love.

In the evening of her young life, Thérèse looked back on her past, and made this touching declaration:

> Your love has gone before me, and it has grown with me, and now it is
> an abyss whose depths I cannot fathom. Love attracts love, and, my
> Jesus, my love leaps towards yours; it would like to fill the abyss that
> attracts it, but alas! it is not even like a drop of dew lost in the ocean!
> For me to love you as you love me, I would have to borrow your own
> love, and then only would I be at rest. (C 35 r; Au 256)

We must draw three conclusions from the foregoing:

(1) Essentially, our love is required to allow God's greater love to triumph. It must gradually elicit the truth that God loves us freely, first and mercifully.

(2) We must accept ourselves in the light of truth: what we are and what we can become, no more and no less; and we must acknowledge our real and inevitable insufficiency. We have to remember that humility is a basic aspect of Thérèse's way.

(3) Of itself, love will never reach its desired goal. Even if it never failed, it could never return God's love *in kind*. We shall always be God's debtors, and that is why hope is so important an element in the development of our spiritu-

ality. All that remains is the prayer: 'Lord, let your love
grow in me. Provide me with what is lacking in my love for
you. Fill my empty hands, give me your own heart.'

This is the inward process we have observed at crucial stages of
Thérèse's journey: her discovery of the 'little way' (1894); her
offering to merciful Love (1895); and the phase represented by
the B manuscript (1896). In fact, the same movement is
discernible in almost all areas of her life. In several poems, for
example, she stressed the nature of her hope:

> Remember that on earth I want
> To console you for the forgetfulness of sinners.
> My only Love, grant my prayer.
> Ah! give me a thousand hearts to love you.
> But that is still too little, Jesus, Beauty Supreme.
> Give me your divine Heart Itself to love you.
> Lord, my burning desire,
> At each moment,
> Remember.
> (PN 24; p. 130)

> It's your love, Jesus, that I crave.
> It's your love that has to transform me.
> Put in my heart your consuming flame,
> And I'll be able to bless you and love you.
> Yes, I'll be able to love you and bless you
> As they do in Heaven.
> I'll love you with that very love
> With which you have loved me, Jesus Eternal Word
> (PN 41; p. 173)

Love can strive to reach God with all the ardour at its disposal,
but 'I may have done the planting and Apollos the watering, but
it was God who made the seed grow! The planter and the
waterer are nothing compared with him who gives life to the
seed. Planter and waterer are alike insignificant, though each
shall be rewarded according to his particular work' (1 Cor. 3: 6–
7). In spite of all imaginable efforts, we can only hope with

complete confidence that God himself will grant us full resemblance to him and full participation in his perfect love. We have every reason to hope that this will happen.

At the very end of his life, the desert mystic and Little Brother Charles de Foucauld wrote to Mme de Bondy: 'How true it is to say that we shall never love enough. But God, who knows of what clay we are molded, and who loves us much more than a mother loves her child, has told us (which means that he who does not lie has told us), that he will not reject whoever wishes to come to him.'

Drawn by His Mercy

On one occasion, when in the thick of a youthful trial, Thérèse had been vouchsafed a very happy experience:

> O my Jesus, it is perhaps an illusion but it seems to me that you cannot fill a soul with more love than the love with which you have filled mine ... here on earth. I cannot conceive a greater immensity of love than the one which it has pleased you to give me freely, *without any merit on my part*. (C 35 r; Au 256)

At another time, when choosing the most beautiful ear of grain from a sheaf she was holding, Thérèse had said: 'This ear is the picture of my soul: God has laden me with graces for myself and for many others' (DE 286).

The same experience also illumined her concept of God (which is wholly consonant with all Jesus' teachings on the subject), and disclosed what God expected from her:

> I understand ... that all souls cannot be the same, that it is necessary there be different types in order to honor each of God's perfections in a particular way. To me he has granted his *infinite Mercy*, and *through it* I contemplate and adore the other divine perfections! ... All these divine perfections appear to be resplendent, *with love*, even his justice (and perhaps this even more so than the others) seems to me clothed in *love*. ... What a sweet joy it is to think that God is *just*, i.e., that he takes into account our weakness, that he is perfectly aware of our fragile nature. What should I fear then? (A 83 v; Au 180)

From then on, Scripture conveyed that divine goodness to her. Psalms 23 ('The Lord is my shepherd') and 103 ('Bless the Lord, my soul') would seem to have been Thérèse's favourites in the Psalter. She had now come to understand so much more proficiently what she had thought at the outset of her religious life when she saw Jesus as a king asking for the hand of a village maiden, as she told Marie Guérin in a letter: 'You give me the impression of a little country girl to whom a powerful king should come and ask her to marry him' (LT 109; LC 130).

Now she devoted her love to God's supremely tender love, offered to us in Jesus' humanity, through his life, death, resurrection and presence in the Eucharist.

She was profoundly aware of the Easter mystery: Jesus is alive; he is close to us; he restores us to life:

> I understand and I know from experience 'that the Kingdom of God is within you.' Jesus has no need of books or teachers to instruct souls; he teaches without the noise of words. Never have I heard him speak, but I feel that he is within me at each moment; he is guiding and inspiring me with what I must say and do. (A 83 v; Au 179)

> I have frequently noticed that Jesus doesn't want me to lay up *provisions*: he nourishes me at each moment with a totally new food; I find it within me without knowing how it is there. I believe it is Jesus himself hidden in the depths of my poor little heart: he is giving me the grace of acting within me, making me think of everything He wants me to do at that moment. (A 76 r; Au 165)

> More than ever I understand that the smallest events of our lives are conducted by God; he is the one who makes us desire and who grants our desires. (LT 201; LC 171)

Here, of course, Thérèse echoes the words of St Paul: 'For it is God who is at work within you, giving you the will and the power to achieve his purpose' (Phil. 2: 13). This will had been alive within Thérèse for a long time. She looked to God for the power to be renewed every day. As to the way in which that power should be sought and, once bestowed, should be exercised, her entire programme is set forth in her bedside book, the New Testament:

> ... my way is all confidence and love. I do not understand souls who fear a Friend so tender. At times, when I am reading certain spiritual treatises in which perfection is shown through a thousand obstacles, surrounded by a crowd of illusions, my poor little mind quickly tires; I close the learned book that is breaking my head and drying up my heart, and I take up Holy Scripture. Then all seems luminous to me; a single word uncovers for my soul infinite horizons, perfection seems simple to me, I see it is sufficient to recognize one's nothingness and to abandon oneself as a child into God's arms. (LT 226; LC 178)

Whenever she read the New Testament, Thérèse was instantly touched by God's mercy made manifest in the person of Jesus:

> I have only to cast a glance in the Gospels and immediately I breathe in the perfumes of Jesus' life, and I know on which side to run. I don't hasten to the first place but to the last; rather than advance like the Pharisee, I repeat, filled with confidence, the publican's humble prayer. Most of all I imitate the conduct of Magdalen; her astonishing or rather her loving audacity which charms the Heart of Jesus also attracts my own. Yes, I feel it; even though I had on my conscience all the sins that can be committed, I would go, my heart broken with sorrow, and throw myself into Jesus' arms, for I know how much he loves the prodigal child who returns to him. (C 36 v; Au 258–9)

More than once she quotes Jesus' words: 'It is not the fit and flourishing who need the doctor, but those who are ill ... In any case I did not come to invite the "righteous" but the "sinners"' (Matt. 9: 12–13).

As an echo of the parable of the lost sheep, the following advice to Céline cannot fail to touch our hearts:

> ... do not fear, the poorer you are the more Jesus will love you. He will go far, very far, in search of you, if at times you wander off a little. (LT 211; LC 172)

Jesus is pleased with little Céline to whom he gave himself for the first time thirteen years ago. He is more proud of what he is doing in her soul, of her littleness and her poverty, than he is proud of having created millions of suns and the expanse of the heavens. (LT 227; LC 178)

Jesus resembles his Father! 'Our' Father, he taught us to say, and this would fill Thérèse with happiness. Indeed, one day Céline had gone in to see her sister who was busy sewing while remaining very recollected. 'What are you thinking of?' asked Céline. 'I'm meditating on the Lord's Prayer', answered Thérèse. 'It is so sweet to call God our Father.' Tears glistened in her eyes as she said this.

Three Comparisons

Three comparisons may serve to show how Thérèse grew in holiness.

A flight into space. First, if we compare God to an expanding universe, we may say that humanity is allowed to penetrate to its centre by virtue of God's own love (for God is Love). But as soon as human love for God seems to grow and to draw humankind deeper into the centre, the latter seems to recede accordingly, thwarting human attempts to advance towards it.

Even though God becomes increasingly lovable and desirable to those who love God more and more, the more they imagine that they are actually in possession of God, the more painfully aware they must become that God is somehow less accessible to them. Even if those in question are allowed entry to the life of grace that is the divine life, participate in that life, and want to possess God more abundantly, because God's centre is 'dynamic' he still eludes them.

In fact, the more rapidly we seem to move ahead in search of God, the more surely God seems to withdraw, and thus remains out of reach. Augustine describes the situation very appositely when he says: 'God is more intimately present to me than I to myself, but he is also higher above me than that which is already above me.'

All comparisons fail in the promised adequacy and the

foregoing is no exception. Of course, there is no 'centre' in God. When we live the love of God, we are already *in* him, for he is indivisible. The point of the illustration is that, through the growing love with which God communicates himself to us, we become increasingly aware that he can always, and *should* always, be loved more and more. Our love is therefore in perpetual motion, for its goal is always beyond its grasp. It is a constant emergence from self, an unending exodus.

Even if we were to exploit all the occasions and possibilities of loving God offered to us, we could never do so adequately or worthily. Nevertheless, we can and should pray that God will make the impossible possible by fully communicating his own love to us in, as it were, a single movement. This would prompt a greater desire to love in us, for the more of his love God gives us so that we can use it to love him in return, the more intense our desire to love him in return becomes.

That was what happened to Thérèse. The more she loved the more she wanted to love. Thérèse seems to smile when she compares her concept of holiness when she was fourteen years old with her views as an adult:

> At the beginning of my spiritual life when I was thirteen or fourteen, I used to ask myself what I would have to strive for later on because I believed it was quite impossible for me to understand perfection better; I learned very quickly since then that the more one advances, the more one sees the goal is still far off. And now I am simply resigned to see myself always imperfect and in this I find my joy. (A 74 r; Au 158)

By falling short of her goal as she advanced, Thérèse had learned she would never succeed in loving by her own power. She saw how her actual love never corresponded to her dreams. It would always have to spring from hope, hope in God alone.

From summit to summit. The second analogy that comes to mind is that of a winding trail leading to a mountain peak. We know from the accounts amateur climbers have given us of their experiences that they are liable to suffer from illusions (but also exaltations) when climbing mountains. They might see a summit looming ahead and immediately conclude they are almost there. But they have scarcely reached it when another, even higher, one appears. Thus it continues, one after the other, until they come to the very last one.

This image might be applied to the spiritual life, but with the difference that there is no final summit in the distance. A fervent soul will always find new heights to be scaled, for God is always just a little 'beyond' our capabilities. To love God 'as' he loves us is, of course, a dream. It is a reality beyond our attainment if only because we can never 'become' God. We are created in God's 'image', and no more than that (Gen. 1: 26). Although we participate in God's being and are united to him, there is a difference and a distance between us. But we must not lose heart for, if there is a dilemma here, there is a way out of it. Thérèse reveals the solution as part of her own daily practice, for she shows us that all we need do is to ask God to bridge the gap by descending to our level and then taking us up to his own level.

In this context we encounter Thérèse's characteristic metaphor of the eagle and the little bird. An individual may possess the 'eyes and heart' of an eagle, that is, its insight and love to the point of folly, but not its 'eagle wings'. Then there is all the more reason to depend on the eagle to swoop down effortlessly and carry the little bird away to its mountain eyrie; to rely, therefore, on the 'adorable Eagle' who will eventually bear Thérèse to his nest and fastness in the empyrean.

Even the holiest love can never love God as he deserves to be loved. We must all accept our innate poverty. We must learn to hope and trust in God's compassionate understanding and readiness to give himself and supplement our natural help-lessness. This hope is no dead-end. It is love on the move; love that is constantly growing and flourishing. Hope is love in the process of becoming. Without hope love would suffocate. St John of the Cross says that love can renounce everything for the sake of the Beloved apart from the desire continually to grow, possess and love the Beloved more:

> Why takest Thou not the heart that Thou hast spoiled through love, in order to fill it and satisfy it and accompany it and heal it, giving it perfect rest and a perfect abode in Thyself? However complete the

agreement between it and the Beloved, the loving soul cannot fail to
desire the recompense and wages of its love, for the sake of which
recompense it serves the Beloved; and otherwise its love would not be
true; for the wages and recompense of love are naught else, nor can it
desire aught else, than greater love, until it attains to perfection of love;
for love confers no payment save of itself. ... So, then, the soul that is
enkindled in the love of God desires the fulfilment and perfection of
love in order to find complete refreshment there, as the servant wearied
with the summer desires the refreshment of the shade ... the soul that
loves awaits not the end of its labour, but the end of its work. For its
work is to love, and of this work, which is to love, the soul awaits the
end and termination, which is the perfection and fulfilment of loving
God. Until this is fulfilled for it, the soul is ever in the form described
by Job ... holding the days and months as empty and counting the
nights as wearisome and tedious for itself ... the soul that loves God
must not claim or hope for any other guerdon for its services save the
perfection of loving God. (St John of the Cross: *Spiritual Canticle*, 9: 7)

Hope has only one aim: to grow increasingly disinterested by
becoming able to give more and more of itself. Hope is like a
plant that blossoms from the compost, that is, from the soil of
love, and bears within itself all the life-bearing sap derived from
that source. Hope is born of the love that engendered it and is
only the most emphatic expression yet of a love that it longs to
raise to a higher level.

Thérèse often used the words 'hope', 'trust' or 'confidence',
and 'surrender' or 'abandonment' interchangeably, and she
would seem to have referred to her hope as 'trust' when she
wished to describe a greater degree of intimacy on her part and a
greater certainty of being heard. Thérèse trusted in God's
fidelity. She banked on his love, pledged herself to his
'philanthropy' (Tt 3: 4), and gambled on his goodness.

Her trust was already a song of praise and gave thanks in
advance for what she hoped to receive. It also indicated her love
of her neighbours, whom she served with increasing generosity
as her love matured. Thérèse prayed confidently: 'I hope to
receive you from yourself for yourself and for all humankind.'
Nevertheless, she did not live her trust as a form of guarantee
against the suffering and darkness that she would inevitably meet

with. Of course her confidence gave her 'the full assurance of hope until the end, so that you may not be sluggish, but imitators of those who through faith and patience inherit the promises' (Heb. 6: 8), although she would always need to seek protection and encouragement for even this full assurance.

Ultimately, authentic trust does not give way under the weight of our indecision and vacillation, even though there are times when we can only believe in hope 'against hope' (Rom. 4: 18). Hope is indeed a source of dynamic life, which encourages us to forget ourselves completely, for it breaks through present bounds and allows us a broader vision and understanding of the future.

Trust also calls for detachment and self-renunciation. It enables us to become the new persons we long to be, although we have to carry on struggling with the old selves that in certain ways we still are, in spite of all our good intentions and resolutions.

Thérèse has often been called the 'saint of love'. Perhaps it would be more appropriate to think of her as the 'saint of super-love'. By this, I mean the saint of a form of hope that aspires to something beyond the initial limited and temporary gift of self; the saint of a kind of hope that looks ahead to that greater, definitive and infinite gift that only God can offer. Thérèse's love never settled for the status quo but cried out 'Not yet!', for she was always aware of her gradual progression towards God, and always looking for opportunities to become more loving.

The confidence we learn about through Thérèse is a synthesis of the best aspects of theological life. It springs from faith in God's goodness, flows through the channel of hope, and empties into that ultimate love to which she constantly aspired to be united more intensely. St Ambrose talks of a 'sacred circuit' between hope and love. Love brings in hope; hope yields more love; and a more ardent love leads to new hope. This renewed hope is then both an expression of love and a plea to be further graced by God. And so, throughout our lives, we advance from love to hope and hope to love, forever scaling new heights till the day of our final union with God, when, after our long journey on the 'little way', we shall be enlightened and illumined in glory.

Even now, however, God hears us as we hope. We have only to say Yes to him in order to become more aware of his wonderful goodness, to rise to his level, and to become more open and receptive to the conditions that will ennoble and sanctify us. His Spirit is at work when he invites us to be strong and courageous in him. Years may pass before any change becomes noticeable in such traits as a peaceful exterior, untiring good will, a joy stemming from an acknowledgement of God's fatherhood, or the certainty that our faults and failures, if we repent of them, are mere drops of water in the furnace of divine love. In spite of our poverty (indeed, thanks to our poverty), if we persevere in hope we shall be much more 'of God'. Moreover, in God's own good time, and after a long life of hope, he might allow some small 'Christmas grace' to burst forth in our lives, as he did for Thérèse.

Thérèse knew how God's life could lie hidden below the surface of a human psyche and temperament, and that some souls were much closer to God than might be apparent if they were judged merely by their struggles and inhibitions. 'What we think of as negligence', Thérèse wrote, 'is very often heroism in the eyes of God' (PO 1755). She warned Céline: 'On the last day, you will be astonished to see your sisters freed from all their imperfections, and they will appear as "great saints"' (CSG 108). Although such 'little souls' might pass unnoticed and have nothing to boast about, they are great in the eyes of God, for in their poverty they are full of hope.

Love or hope? Which will have the last word? Thérèse's three autobiographical manuscripts all end with the word 'love', from which we might conclude that love provided the main impetus in Thérèse's spirituality. But did she mean love as achievement, or as ideal and, therefore, as hope?

In a way, the last word on earth can only be 'hope', for true love of its nature leads to love, and desires it increasingly. On the other hand, love can aspire to more love only through hope. Moreover, love needs hope to beseech heaven for its fulfilment and to grow and expand beyond its own limitations. When asked what her little way consisted of, Thérèse replied: 'It is the way of trust, of total abandonment' (DE 257), built upon a 'loving confidence' (LT 261) with confidence as the seed and love as its fruit. In the end, we might say that even if hope is not the last, it must be the next to last word. We shall receive the last word from Jesus when we meet in glory. This word will be veritable Love, the Word of God himself, who is LOVE.

A bridge is a third metaphor that might help us to understand Thérèse's doctrine. In spite of all her efforts, Thérèse realized only too well that she had not yet reached the fullness of love. She was at the edge of an 'abyss', or chasm (C 35 r), which she wanted to cross in order to respond to her Beloved. The problem was how to bridge it.

Fortunately, there was a solid pier on either side of this chasm. One represented her humble acceptance of her incomplete and helpless state; the other God's infinite mercy, in which she believed with her whole heart. Humility and faith in God's mercy are essential components of hope. Surely, then, the bridge of 'loving confidence' described in the foregoing would enable Thérèse to meet her Lord? But it would be more theologically appropriate to conceive of God himself as leaping over the chasm to meet Thérèse, shower his gifts on her, and bear her swiftly to his side. Then God himself would be the bridge to his love.

Thérèse was convinced that this God of love would constantly increase the zeal of his poor creature's desire to love him. What she had written of the prayer of petition could be applied to hope as well, for petition is the language of hope:

> Ah! it is prayer, it is sacrifice which give me all my strength, these are the invincible weapons which Jesus has given me. (C 24 v; Au 240–1)

> How great is the power of *Prayer*! One could call it a Queen who has at each instant free access to the King and who is able to obtain whatever she asks. (C 25 r; Au 242)

> A scholar has said: '*Give me a lever and a fulcrum and I will lift the world.*' What Archimedes was not able to obtain, for his request was not directed by God and was only made from a material viewpoint, the saints have obtained in all its fullness. The Almighty has given them as *fulcrum: HIMSELF ALONE*; as *lever: PRAYER* which burns with a fire

of love. And it is in this way that they have lifted the world; it is in this way that the saints still militant lift it, and that, until the end of time, the saints to come will lift it. (C 36 r–v; Au 258)

Jesus himself taught us to express our hope in the Lord's Prayer, which will certainly prove to be effective. Thérèse stressed the importance of remembering that Jesus has shown us how reasonable and justifiable it is to hope:

> ... through beautiful parables, and often even without using this means so well known to the people, he teaches us that it is enough to knock and it will be opened, to seek in order to find, and to hold out one's hand humbly to receive what is asked for. He also says that everything we ask the Father in his name, he will grant it. No doubt, it is because of this teaching that the Holy Spirit, before Jesus' birth, dictated this prophetic prayer: 'Draw me, we shall run.' (C 35 v; Au 257)

Thérèse's sisters testified that there were no limits to her hope. And, to be sure, she had written: 'Jesus was very right in saying that there is no greater love.... How would he allow himself to be overcome in generosity?' (LT 226; LC 178); and:

> To limit your desires and your hopes is to misunderstand God's infinite goodness! My infinite desires are my wealth, and for me the words of Jesus will come true: 'To the one who possesses it will be given and given in abundance!' (PA 1352)

She would often repeat the words of St John of the Cross: 'We receive from God insofar as we hope in him.'

But nothing illustrates the transforming effect of trust as clearly as Thérèse's own life. Her 'elevator' worked perfectly. She experienced the incursions of God's mercy in her own existence. Her fidelity grew immensely and her love of her neighbour became unrestricted. She also instilled the same confidence in her young charges in every possible way, and used the metaphor of a toddler still unable to mount the bottom step:

> Agree to be that little child. Through the practice of all the virtues, raise

your little foot to scale the stairway of holiness. You won't succeed in reaching the first step, but God requires you only to demonstrate your good will. Soon, conquered by your futile efforts, he will descend himself, gather you up in his arms, and carry you off to his kingdom for ever. (PA 1403)

To Sister Marie of the Trinity, who wished she were just a mite more energetic, she replied:

And if God wanted you to be weak and powerless as a child, do you believe you would have fewer merits? Agree to stumble at every step, even to fall, to carry your crosses weakly; love your helplessness, your soul will benefit more from it than if, sustained by grace, you accomplished with enthusiasm heroic actions which would fill your soul with personal satisfaction and pride. (PA 2129)

Of herself she remarked simply:

... you can see that I am *a very little soul* and that I can offer God only *very little things*. It often happens that I allow these little sacrifices which give such peace to the soul to slip by; this does not discourage me, for I put up with having a little less peace and I try to be more vigilant on another occasion. (C 31 r; Au 250)

Works or Trust?

Of course, the foregoing might lead some people to think that Thérèse stressed the importance of trust to the detriment of works, and that she tried to encourage the adoption of a mystique of weakness.

Once more we are faced with the perennial paradox of a God who deserves complete fidelity from his creatures, yet favors the imperfect and acknowledges their poverty. The same paradox appears throughout the Gospels in the theme of the redemption of the lowly. This co-existence of personal responsibility and of God's overflowing mercy remains a mystery.

Many of Thérèse's own expressions are similarly paradoxical: 'Love is paid only by love' but 'the proof of love is in our works'

(B 4 r). Yet elsewhere she claims that 'Jesus does not need our works but only our love' (B 1 v). She insisted, however, that 'my way is not a form of "quietism"; it is not a passive surrender' (PA 1358). Nevertheless, she did want to die 'with empty hands' and admitted: 'If I had sought to collect merits, I would be desperate at this late hour' (CSG 57). Love was a 'torrent' that left nothing in its wake (CSG 12), but when God was ready to recompense her for her loving deeds: 'He will be very much embarrassed in my case. I haven't any works! Well then. He will reward me according to his own works' (DE 43).

Thérèse neither recommended activism nor tolerated tepidity. At the time of her 'oblation to merciful love' she had written: 'It is not always energy that one lacks in becoming a saint, and yet it is a most necessary virtue; with energy one can easily reach the summit of perfection' (LT 178; LC 162).

When she referred to the grace she had received at Christmas as a merciful gift, she added: 'Many souls will say: "But I don't have the strength to make such a sacrifice." Then let them do what I did: make a great effort!' (DE 142).

She liked to repeat Jesus' reminder to us that no one would enter the kingdom of Heaven by crying 'Lord, Lord' but rather 'by doing God's will' (C 11 v). But she was sure that it was just as important to stress the basic role of 'good will' (A 45 v; CSG 22).

This seeming paradox is partially resolved when we analyse Thérèse's scale of values. She thought of the true inward value of an action as something derived from an individual's love and not from the importance of that action 'in itself' or in a specific context. Love ennobles all things, and without it the greatest accomplishment is worth nothing in God's eyes:

I understood that without *love* all works are nothing, even the most dazzling, such as raising the dead to life and converting peoples. (A 81 v; Au 175)

It is not the value nor even the apparent holiness of our actions that counts, but only the love which we put into them. (CSG 65)

To think beautiful lofty thoughts, to write books or to write lives of saints, does not equal one act of love of God, not even the act of answering the bell when it disturbs you. (CSG 10)

Essentially, this love is a matter of the right intentions of the heart, of the will to do what is pleasing to God even if the action is never actually completed. The main thing is to act with much love; to sustain that love even if the intended goal is not reached; to maintain one's good will; and to try, try again. All this may betray human inadequacy, but it also expresses true love and appeals to the mercy of God.

When Thérèse spoke of the necessity of works, she was not thinking of those that stand out as brilliant or remarkable. She was wary of feats of physical mortification and rejected all desires for extraordinary mystical phenomena. She was convinced that such experiences were not proper to 'little souls' but belonged to spiritualities other than her 'little way'. She preferred the purity and disinterestedness of faith: 'It is so sweet to serve God in the midst of trials. We have but this life to live by faith' (CSG 156).

Now we can understand more effectively why Thérèse tended to focus her fidelity to love on numerous small occasions of everyday life that offer opportunities for action that are available to each one of us. She knew that there was room for heroism in all those normal events that occur in the course of each individual's life.

When Thérèse described (in the B manuscript) how she wanted to fulfill every possible vocation with love, she established a plan of action:

Yes, my Beloved, this is how my life will be consumed. I have no other means of proving my love for you other than that of strewing flowers, that is, not allowing one little sacrifice to escape, not one look, one word, profiting by all the smallest things and doing them through love. I desire to suffer for love and even to rejoice through love; and in this way I shall strew flowers before your throne. I shall not come upon one without *unpetalling* it for you. While I am strewing my flowers, I shall sing, for could one cry while doing such a joyous action? I shall sing even when I must gather my flowers in the midst of thorns, and my song will be all the more melodious in proportion to the length and sharpness of the thorns. (B 4 r–v; Au 196–7)

Minor things; matters of no consequence; 'fragile petals of no value'; 'nothings'; a minor sacrifice here; a look, a word, a smile there: all these are things that speak of absolute fidelity. A desire to profit from 'everything', to allow 'no' occasion to slip by, but a radical attitude inspired by love alone: 'for you', 'out of love'. Thérèse's agenda is profoundly joyful to an extent that not even suffering can overshadow. But it is only an agenda: an orientation and a task. Thérèse admitted that she is just a 'feeble little bird', an 'imperfect little creature' who from time to time 'lets herself be distracted from her unique occupation', and acknowledges her petty 'faults' and 'infidelities' (B 5 r). Her astonishing good will always encountered the equally wonderful mercy of God! How Thérèse would have enjoyed the following parable from Rabindranath Tagore's *Sacred Songs*, which stresses the wealth of love that a minor, apparently humble, gesture can contain:

I had gone a-begging from door to door on the village road
when your golden carriage appeared like a dream in the distance.
Astonished, I asked myself if this could be the King of Kings.

My expectations rose very high.
I thought that my difficult times were coming to an end at last
I looked everywhere for the gifts that would be lavished
without the asking,
and for the riches strewn around me in the dust.

Then the carriage stopped near me.
Your gaze met mine and you alighted with a smile.
The happiness of my life had come at last.
But then you suddenly extended your right hand, and said:
'What do you have to give me?'

Ah! This was a royal farce,
this holding of your hand outstretched before a beggar!

Confused and undecided, I slowly dug into my sack

and took out a small, a very small grain of wheat
and gave it to you.

Imagine my surprise when at the end of the day
I emptied my sack on the ground
and found a small, a very small nugget of gold
in that miserable pile.
I cried bitterly and wished I had had the courage
to give you everything I had.

Works or trust? Thérèse offers us a well-balanced agenda: we love as much as we can, and we try to prove our love by our actions; but whenever we do not succeed as we would wish, we simply trust in God's infinite mercy. Nevertheless, whatever the level our love has reached (and we must remember that this love is, first and foremost, God's gift entrusted to our responsible care), it must try to express itself in the form of actions. As it grows we should make an even greater effort to prove its adequacy in the practical instances of our everyday lives. This constant fidelity, this continuous attempt to accord with God's love by means of his grace provides the basis for our spontaneous trust in him.

In all her references to the necessity of works, Thérèse was very careful to give full credit to the Lord's mercy, and to belittle her own contribution. She explained to one of her novices that her little way was nothing but the All and Nothing of St John of the Cross, and that we arrive at the All by way of the Nothing. She observed that this All himself came to meet us, and that ultimately our complete giving of self in return had to come from him:

Climb? God wants to make you *come down*! *Acquire?* Rather, say *lose*! (CSG 26)

You'd like to have already arrived; you are astonished at your falling. One must always expect to fall. (CSG 30)

... we must consent to remain always poor and without strength, and this is the difficulty. (LT 197; LC 170)

Those who are poor in spirit, in Thérèse's view, are not anxiously preoccupied with the results of their spiritual efforts. They do not want to see and understand everything, and do not count on success. They live on faith and trust and do not worry about progress, for they are entirely committed in love – committed to God's care.

Thérèse even wished to renounce all her merits. It was as if she sensed the danger of claiming self-sufficiency as if it were some kind of right to boast of one's good deeds before God. She had become a stranger to spiritual ambition and compensation. She did not want to reduce her utter dependence on God's mercy in any way. In the end, that contributed to her greatest merit. It led her to live out of God's hand, as it were, and to accept in blind trust whatever he asked of her or sent her, even by way of suffering. Her self-surrender in this sense was a sustained act of trust in the hands of the Beloved, from whom she expected all things, including his merciful intervention.

In the last analysis, what I presented earlier as a paradoxical aspect of Thérèse's life and thought remains paradoxical. Nevertheless, the paradox is a matter of complementary attitudes: of striving as if everything depended on oneself, yes, but in the continual expectation that one's efforts will be crowned by God alone. Thérèse united the two apparent paradoxes in the synthetic whole of an injunction to do one's best and let God do the rest:

> One must do everything in one's power. One must give without counting the cost, constantly renounce oneself, in a word give proof of one's love by all the good deeds within one's reach. But, really, since all of this is of little value . . . it is necessary, when we have done everything we thought we should do, to admit that we are 'useless servants' (Luke 17: 18), hoping all the same that God will give us through his grace everything we desire. (CSG 157)

Thérèse could no longer tolerate being rich in any area:

> Even if I had accomplished all the works of St Paul, I would consider

myself 'a useless servant,' but that is precisely what gives me such joy, for, having nothing, I shall receive everything from God. (DE 67)

In that tension between activity and self-surrender, her heart was already inclining towards the latter; and that comprised both her charisma and the secret of the encouragement that flowed from her. The very last sentence in her autobiography – *happily* the last, for the dying Thérèse could no longer write – shows precisely how her confidence was based not on her own virtue but on *God's* goodness:

It is not because God, in his anticipating mercy, has preserved my soul from mortal sin that I go to him with confidence and love. (C 36 v) [Here Thérèse insisted that Mother Agnes add this thought: 'Really tell them ... that if I had committed all possible crimes, I would always have the same confidence; I feel that this whole multitude of offenses would be like a drop of water thrown into a fiery furnace.'] (DE 89)

A well-known definition of holiness has been attributed to Thérèse. In all likelihood it was Mother Agnes who put the actual words on Thérèse's lips, but the inspiration is perfectly 'Thérèsian':

Holiness is not this or that practice, it consists in a disposition of the heart which makes us humble and small in God's arms, aware of our weakness, and trusting to a daring degree, in the Father's goodness. (Cf. DE, French edition, p. 235)

Thérèse's road to sanctity underwent a remarkable evolution. To use an analogy, we could say that, at first, her hand was held with palm downward and fingers clenched, seeking to grasp as best they could. Then, with the passage of time and a change of attitude and perspective, her fingers relaxed gradually and eventually released their hold, while her hand turned until her palm was outstretched, ready to offer and to receive much in return. It took Thérèse almost her entire lifetime to reach this point.

At the Heart of Christianity

In her writings, although still a young Carmelite, Thérèse expressed some very profound theological views on the relationship between God and his creatures. She did not happen on them through formal study but discovered them personally. She did so through her own process of growth under the guiding light of the Holy Spirit, to whom she had surrendered herself with an unusually highly nuanced sensibility. She hit on the heart of the Christian message almost without the knowledge she could have gleaned from the conventional sources open to her. Then she lived the essence of that message profoundly. But she also clarified it, and related it to the central issue of Pauline theology, with which she integrated it. She might also be said to have made the Church aware of the possibilities of this particular amalgam.

In his letters to the Galatians and to the Romans, Paul showed the inappropriateness of the Mosaic Law to a Pharisee (standing for a major aspect of contemporary Judaism as Paul conceived of it) in search of holiness. Its statutes were so numerous, rigorous, exacting and confusing that it was next to impossible to observe them faithfully or even adequately. Moreover, such an individual lacked the moral power to do so effectively, for he was forced to rely on his own spiritual resources. Nevertheless, he tried to observe the Law literally, but eventually, in spite of all his efforts, became legalistic and, in the end, self-righteous.

Paul pointed out with an almost polemical insistence that this self-reliant attitude was fundamentally opposed to that of a Christian, who was invited to expect redemption from Another: from, that is, God. According to Paul, the type of person he characterized as a Pharisee believed that he had to be self-sufficient in order to become a saint. Holiness was the work of *his* hands. His preference was for works for which he would receive all the credit and the glory. Such self-seeking was not proper or acceptable to a Christian, who could properly desire only a reaction and a response, through grace, to God's presence in his or her life.

Through the teachings of Christ and the gift of the Holy

Spirit, Christians believed above all in a loving acceptance of, and abandonment to, God's love as the basis and springboard for their own works. Once impelled by this divine grace, Christian neighbourly love became the due response to God's grace in their soul. This complete change from self-dependency to God-dependency for the purpose of one's sanctification was a radical departure from the Pharisaical concept (as described by Paul) of a relationship with God and neighbor. Thereafter God would work through the human mediation of Christ, the Way, the Truth and the Life, and of the Holy Spirit, now and henceforth made more abundantly available to human souls.

Paul saw and preached Christ as putting an end to the Old Law of personal sanctification. He conceived of Christ as perfecting the Law with superabundant grace, thus nailing to the cross (as he put it) the powerlessness of the Law. Jesus not only emphasized the importance of love as the first and greatest commandment, but offered us his own Spirit. This Spirit became available in superabundance through that breath of life we call 'grace', which gives us the capacity to live according to the new Law.

Grace alone sanctifies us. The Holy Spirit gives us this grace at baptism, then infuses and suffuses our lives with love, and urges us to draw near to the Father. The love of Christ, says Paul, impels us. It is infinitely faithful to us, and nothing can separate us from it if *we* too are faithful.

Grace is essentially of God, from whom it comes, for it was merited by Jesus' death and resurrection. We open ourselves to the action of grace through faith, and Christ, faith and grace are the essential elements of the new axis round which Christian holiness now turns. We do not save ourselves. Christ saves us. We are weak, but we can nevertheless 'glory' in our weakness because it is through that same weakness that the glory of God is made manifest. Is this conditional? Yes, we have to acknowledge that weakness. Only then can we turn from ourselves, and open ourselves to God and to his action in us.

In a certain sense, Thérèse too had to find a way to solve this Pauline problem. It was a painful process. Like St Paul, she first had to experience the failure of her attempt to reach holiness by her own efforts, as it were, before she could claim a victory.

When Paul first met Christ on the road to Damascus, he was left with an impression he would never forget. He was thrown half-senseless to the ground, and got up again, though blinded by the light surrounding him. He had bitten the dust literally and figuratively. As he observed, neither he nor the Law was in the right, but only Jesus whom he was persecuting. Darkness and light, a fiasco and a revelation, a crisis and the prospect of deliverance were the paradoxical results of God's intervention, and would lead to a gradual change in his thinking and convictions.

Thérèse experienced a similar reversal. A first 'conversion' prompted her to dream of an idealized sanctity: 'Love without any limit but you.' But her ethic of perfection gradually came to disturb and even torture her. Yet the experience of her insufficiency and the knowledge of God which surpasses all things were bound to develop until she confronted a dilemma to be resolved only by capitulating in one of two ways. She could say: 'My dream of infinite love was a youthful illusion vanishing in the face of reality. I shall renounce my ideal, lower my sights, and temper my aspirations. ...' Or she could proclaim firmly: 'I shall surrender myself to God even more emphatically than before. I shall take the risk of trusting blindly in his strength, which will work for me.'

Thérèse's decision to make the second of these choices was a sign that the Holy Spirit was guiding her. Her second conversion – the more profound of the two – took her from a state of trusting in her own efforts to perseverance in total confidence in God. Fully aware of what she was doing, she handed the work of her sanctification to Jesus, the ultimate banker and bursar of her spiritual investments.

Some time passed before she understood in practice rather than in theory that it was not a matter of her winning the Beloved. It is never a question of our gaining him. Instead the Beloved wants to take the initiative. He wants to give himself. He is neither a fortress to be captured nor a salary to be earned. *He* is the Redeemer; *he* is the Saviour.

Perhaps a certain state of desperation is necessary in order to discover hope. True hope is found beyond the mere condition of dreaming. Only when the heart realizes that dreaming has been transcended by trust can it open up appropriately to the Lord of life and holiness. Only then can the expectations and longings of the heart be effectively all-embracing, active and constant:

> Holiness is much more the fruit of receptivity and self-surrender than of zeal and the practice of virtues. More precisely, practice and effort are indispensable conditions; but they are no more than that, for the truly essential element of holiness is a gift. In the Christian tradition, that gift is known as grace. (Han Fortmann, *Easter Rebirth*)

Here Thérèse enters the very heart of the Gospel. Her 'spiritual childhood' (a formula which she never used herself) consists in living deliberately and thoroughly that spirit of adoption 'into the very family circle of God' when she can 'say with a full heart: "Father, my Father"' (Rom. 8: 15). Her self-offering to God's own mercy is a logical outcome of 'the love of God in Christ Jesus our Lord':

> I have become absolutely convinced that neither death nor life, neither messenger of heaven nor monarch of earth, neither what happens today nor what may happen tomorrow, neither a power from on high nor a power from below, nor anything else in God's whole world has any power to separate us from the love of God in Christ Jesus our Lord! (Rom. 8: 39).

Her 'trust' is the essence of Paul's faith: loving surrender to God's saving grace. Paul's Letter to the Christians at Rome was among Thérèse's favourite readings. She quoted or referred to it a dozen times at least. She kept the following conflated passages from Rom. 4: 46–51 and 3: 21–4 in her breviary:

> Faith is to be reckoned as righteousness to us also. ... Since it is by faith that we are justified, let us grasp the fact that we *have* peace with God through our Lord Jesus Christ. Through him we have confidently entered into this new relationship of grace, and here we take our stand, in happy certainty of the glorious things he has for us in future ... now we are seeing the righteousness of God declared quite apart from the Law ... it is a righteousness imparted to, and operating in, all who have faith in Jesus Christ. ...

Now she knows with certainty and joy that Jesus wants to be our Savior.

Several commentators have noticed the ecumenical tendency of Thérèse's doctrine. This young girl was a deeply believing Catholic, dedicated in obedience to the authority of the Church. In lifestyle and personal behaviour she was immersed in the Catholic life of her time. Nevertheless, the way in which she conceived of the life of faith brought her interestingly close to the Lutheran notion of salvation through faith alone.

~2 7 ~

Your Life in Mine

THE REMAINING YEARS of Thérèse's life were marked by a growing conformity and openness to God's mercy working in her, with regard to her neighbor, her apostolate and her prayer life.

The 'Mysterious Depths' of Neighborly Love

As Thérèse discovered more aspects of the authentic image of God, she became able to read her neighbor's face more accurately. In 1897, the last year of her life, she reached the summit of her love for God and received 'the grace to understand what charity is' (C 11 v).

At one time she appeared to have understood and lived it to perfection in her community. But she readily admitted later: 'I understood it before, it is true, but in an imperfect way' (C 11 v).

The difference was that now Thérèse was particularly sensitive to and impressed by the implications of Jesus' words: ' "Thou shalt love the Lord thy God with all thy heart, and with all thy soul and with all thy mind." This is the first and great commandment. And there is a second like it: "Thou shalt love thy neighbor as thyself" '; and 'Now I am giving you a new command – love one another. Just as I have loved you, so you must love one another' (Matt. 22: 39 and John 13: 24).

As, just as … She always experienced that same desire to be like Jesus in his loving-kindness. Thérèse knew and wrote that, of herself, she would never be capable of producing such an intensity of love. But, since she had discovered her little way, it had seemed that the limits of what was possible had expanded infinitely. Therefore she allowed Jesus to act in her: 'I'm incapable of it; do it yourself in me; I abandon myself entirely to you ...'

That was her great insight in 1897: that Jesus himself loves my neighbor through me.

> Ah, Lord, I know that you don't command the impossible. You know better than I do my weakness, my imperfection, you know very well that never would I be able to love my Sisters as you love them, unless *you*, O my Jesus, *loved them in me*. It is because you wanted to give me this grace that you made your new commandment. Oh! how I love this new commandment since it gives me the assurance that your will is *to love in me* all those you command me to love! Yes, I feel it, when I am charitable, it is Jesus alone who is acting in me, and the more united I am to him, the more also do I love my Sisters. (C 12 v; Au 221)

Thérèse had penetrated and plumbed the 'mysterious depths' of charity (C 18 v). Thérèse and Jesus, who loves her neighbour through her, are but one! Thérèse is the outward expression of Jesus' love for others in her soul. Indeed, not only are Thérèse and Jesus one, but similarly Jesus and her neighbor are also one. At one time her love of her neighbor had been a small stepladder she could use to reach God's love more accurately and promptly: 'I applied myself especially to *loving God*' (C 11 v; A 219). Now her neighbor was neither a stepping stone nor a ladder but the Lord's own reflection. All distances between her and her neighbours had dissolved: she saw 'Jesus hidden in the depths' of others' souls (C 14 r; Au 222), so that the love of Jesus-in-her-heart flowed from person to person to Jesus-in-the-heart-of-her-neighbor, leaving both giver and recipient comforted and full of joy.

The C manuscript of Thérèse's autobiography is a very realistic and shrewd miniature treatise on neighborly charity. It is written with humour and wisdom. What did 'perfect' neighbourly charity mean to Thérèse at this stage of her life?

> Charity consists in bearing with the faults of others, in not being surprised at their weakness, in being edified by the smallest acts of virtue we see them practice. (C 12 r; Au 220)

Nothing could be more positive, nothing more authentic. She also considered herself 'the servant, the slave of others' (C 16; Au 226). Wholly given up to God's work in her, she had decided to 'renounce her very last rights'. In her community, except for the hours of prayer fixed by the schedule, she would devote herself utterly to the service of others whenever charity demanded it and circumstances made it possible. This would certainly enable her to make the greatest possible progress in loving, for:

> Love is nourished only by sacrifices, and the more a soul refuses natural satisfactions, the stronger and more disinterested becomes its tenderness. (C 21 v; Au 237)

True love would not take long to find its most appropriate expression:

> One is obliged at times to refuse a service because of one's duties; but when charity has buried its roots deeply within the soul, it shows itself externally. There is such a delightful way of refusing what cannot be given that the refusal gives as much pleasure as the gift itself. (C 18 r; Au 228)

Therefore Thérèse tried to celebrate others' lives and her own life in one long spiritual banquet. But the devices she used to do this are all small things: the versatile language of her features, hands, words and thoughts:

> I want to be friendly with everybody (and especially with the least amicable Sisters) to give joy to Jesus and respond to the counsel he gives in the Gospel in almost these words: 'When you give a dinner or supper do not invite your friends, or your brethren, or your relatives, or your rich neighbours, lest perhaps they also invite you in return, and a recompense be made to you. But when you give a feast, invite the poor, the crippled, the lame, the blind; and blessed shall you be, because they have nothing to repay you with, your Father who sees in secret will reward you' (Luke 14: 12–14). What banquet could a Carmelite offer her Sisters except a spiritual banquet of loving and joyful charity? (C 28 v; Au 246–7)

Thérèse was already quite ill when she wrote those words. But, wherever she was, and whatever condition she was in, she seemed to reflect the sun's light and warmth. On 8 July 1897, she descended to the infirmary, from which she never returned. Preparation was made to celebrate the rite for the sick – in those days a sign of imminent death. The sadness of the occasion could be felt throughout the house. The next day, perhaps the very day when Thérèse wrote the very last words of her autobiography, Mother Agnes noted:

> Someone had caught a mouse in the infirmary and she made up a whole story about it, asking us to bring her the wounded mouse so she could keep it next to her and have the doctor examine it with a stethoscope. We laughed heartily and she was happy to have distracted us. (DE 84)

Certainly Thérèse was loved in her community, and this was evident from what she wrote – not without a touch of diplomacy – to Mother Marie de Gonzague:

> *Here*, dear Mother, I live without any burdens from the cares of this miserable earth, and have only to accomplish the sweet and easy mission you have confided to me. *Here*, I receive your motherly attention and do not feel the pinch of poverty since I never lack anything. But *here,* above all, I am loved by you and all the Sisters, and this affection is very sweet to me. This is why I dream of a monastery where I shall be unknown, where I would suffer from poverty, the lack of affection, and finally, the exile of the heart. (C 10 r; Au 217–18)

The Soul of the Apostolate

In Carmel Thérèse looked directly to the Lord for inspiration, strength and the life-giving breath of the Spirit that causes the seed to sprout. For Thérèse had a ministry, although she did not have to trudge the highways and byways of the earth in order to pursue it. Pius XI proclaimed her universal patron of the missions and equal to St Francis Xavier, but she is also the undeclared patron of the domestic apostolate: of, that is, the restricted environment in which most people live, whether the home, the locality or the work-place.

Thérèse's immediate environment consisted of twenty-five Sisters, a few correspondents, the friends and relatives who visited her occasionally, a chaplain and confessor, and the physician who looked after her in the infirmary. These were her 'neighbours'. On them and with them she used the various forms of ministry available to her: witnessing to and through her faith, joyful goodness, an attentive ear, the right word at the right moment, and advice and encouragement in her letters. All these means at her disposal were the fruits of her love for Jesus and her zeal for the Father's kingdom.

As unofficial mistress of novices, Thérèse was also able to carry out a highly valuable mission in caring for her five charges. She was their mentor and constant spiritual companion and adviser. She did not succeed with them in every respect, but once she had realized that 'the task was beyond my strength', she listened to the basic intuitions that came from the practice of her little way; then her task became quite simple:

> I threw myself into the arms of God as a little child and, hiding my face in his hair, I said: 'Lord, I am too little to nourish your children; if you wish to give through me what is suitable for each, fill my little hand and without leaving your arms or turning my head, I shall give your treasures to the soul who will come and ask for nourishment. If she finds it according to her taste, I shall know it is not to me but to you she owes it; on the contrary, if she complains and finds bitter what I present, my peace will not be disturbed, and I shall try to convince her this nourishment comes from you and be very careful not to seek any other for her.' Mother, from the moment I understood that it was impossible for me to do anything by myself, the task you imposed on me no longer appeared difficult. I felt that the only thing necessary was to unite myself more and more to Jesus and that 'all things will be given to you besides.' In fact, never was my hope mistaken, for God saw fit to fill my little hand as many times as it was necessary for nourishing the souls of my Sisters. (C 22 r–v; Au 238)

Of course Thérèse had placed all her talents at the Lord's disposal, and asked him constantly to refine them:

I admit, dear Mother, that if I had depended in the least on my own strength, I would very soon have had to give up. *From a distance* it appears all roses *to do good to souls*, making them love God more and molding them according to one's personal views and ideas. *At close range* it is totally the contrary, the roses disappear; one feels that to do good is as impossible without God's help as to make the sun shine at night. One feels it is absolutely necessary to forget one's likings, one's personal conceptions, and to guide souls along the road which Jesus has traced out for them without trying to make them walk one's own way. (C 22 v; Au 238)

Her own experience had impressed on her the importance of respecting each individual personality in its own right:

I . . . learned very much when I was teaching others. I saw first of all that all souls have very much the same struggles to fight, but they differ so much from each other in other aspects that I have no trouble in understanding what Father Pichon was saying: '*There are really more differences among souls than there are among faces.*' (C 23 v; Au 239–40)

She also knew:

. . . that there are souls for whom [God's] mercy never tires of waiting and to whom he grants his light only by degrees. (C 21 r; Au 236)

Thérèse was well aware that it was pointless to try to anticipate God's own timing.

'*So Intimately United to You*'

Thérèse saw a profound union with Jesus as the indispensable condition for a fruitful apostolate. After ministering to each individual soul, she would bring it and its many needs to the Lord in prayer. She had vast aspirations for all these individuals, for her missionaries and for the universal Church. Sooner or later she had to ask herself how she could possibly serve each and every one of her claimants.

One morning, the light shining from her little way showed her how to escape from her dilemma. The answer was to

surrender herself entirely to Jesus, when he himself would take
care of her difficulties:

> For simple souls there must be no complicated ways; as I am of their
> number, one morning during my thanksgiving, Jesus gave me a simple
> means of accomplishing my mission. He made me understand these
> words of the Canticle of Canticles (The Song of Solomon): '*DRAW*
> *ME, WE SHALL RUN after you in the odor of your ointments.*' O Jesus, it
> is not even necessary to say: '*When drawing me, draw the souls whom I*
> *love!*' This simple statement, 'Draw me' suffices; I understand, Lord,
> that when a soul allows herself to be captivated by the odor of your
> ointments, she cannot run alone, all the souls whom she loves follow in
> her train; this is done without constraint, without effort, it is a natural
> consequence of her attraction for you. Just as a torrent, throwing itself
> with impetuosity into the ocean, drags after it everything it encounters
> in its passage, in the same way, O Jesus, the soul who plunges into the
> shoreless ocean of your love, draws with her all the treasures she
> possesses. (C 33 v–34 r; Au 254)

Thérèse was often distracted during her long hours of prayer,
or fell asleep in spite of fervent efforts to stay awake, but these
physical imperfections never influenced her faith and her trust
in Jesus, who cherished her so profoundly. The solution she
found was to implore him to draw her to him, so that he could
live and pray in her:

> This is my prayer. I ask Jesus to draw me into the flames of his love, to
> unite me so closely to him that he live and act in me. I feel that the
> more the fire of love burns within my heart, the more I shall say: 'Draw
> me'. (C 36 r; Au 257)

Thérèse felt magnetized by Jesus. By night and by day her heart
lost itself in him:

> I do believe I have never been three minutes without thinking of God.
> ... We naturally think of someone we love. (CSG 77)

In her poem of 1895, 'Living on Love', she had written:

Living on Love is living on your life,
Glorious King, delight of the elect.
You live for me, hidden in a host.
I want to hide myself for you, O Jesus!
Lovers must have solitude,
A heart-to-heart lasting night and day.
Just one glance of yours makes my beatitude.
I live on love!
(PN 17; p. 90)

When she was in the infirmary and tuberculosis had affected her whole body, she nevertheless had time to pray, especially during the night. A few weeks before her death, Céline found her with hands joined in prayer and eyes raised to heaven. 'Why are you doing that?' asked Céline. 'You should be trying to sleep.' 'I can't, I'm suffering too much, so I pray.' 'And what do you say to Jesus?' 'I say nothing, *I love him!*' (DE 228).

Jesus was her refuge in storm and tempest, her light in the darkness, and some part of her heaven here on earth:

Heaven for me is feeling within myself the resemblance
Of the God who created me with his Powerful Breath.
Heaven for me is remaining always in his presence,
Calling him my Father and being his child.
In his Divine arms, I don't fear the storm.
Total abandonment is my only law.
Sleeping on his Heart, right next to his Face,
That is Heaven for me!
(PN 32; p. 153)

She always experienced the Lord's Prayer as an enactment of profound emotional appeal, longing and expectation (C 25 v). Her entire spirituality was a living commentary on the petitions Jesus taught us to make to our Father in heaven. Thérèse lived like one of the *anawim*, the poor of Yahweh who looked forward to their salvation, trusting in God; or one of those humble souls who, like Mary, are famished yet filled with good things, for 'He has satisfied the hungry with good things and sent the rich away with empty hands' (Luke 1: 53).

As for the part played by Mary in Thérèse's life, suffice to say that Thérèse loved her from her earliest moments of awareness. Her love for Mary was very tender, as can be seen from her last poem, in which she tried to express the theme 'Why I Love You, O Mary' for the last time.

Thérèse saw Mary as the mother and prototype of all little souls who follow 'the common path' of faith and trust. Nazareth and Lisieux were not so very different. Thérèse may have needed twenty-five stanzas to express her reasons for loving Mary as she did, but they can all be summed up in the final words of the last stanza: 'I am your child':

> Soon I'll hear that sweet harmony.
> Soon I'll go to beautiful Heaven to see you.
> You who came to smile at me in the morning of my life,
> Come smile at me again ... Mother ... It's evening now! ...
> I no longer fear the splendor of your supreme glory.
> With you I've suffered, and now I want
> To sing on your lap, Mary, why I love you,
> And to go on saying that I am your child.
> (PN 54; p. 220)

❦ 8 ❧

A Great Achievement

JESUS SAID: 'Blessed are the poor in spirit: theirs is the Kingdom of Heaven' (Matt. 5: 3). Thérèse was poor in everything, including herself, but rich in God because she trusted in him without any reserve whatsoever: 'Everything is ours', she said. 'Everything is for us, for in Jesus we have everything' (CSG 236).

A Happy Woman

Thérèse knew that God came to her ever more surely as a gift. God was in her heart, and her destiny was in his hands. She already possessed and enjoyed everything in advance. She no longer felt any strong desire for any created thing or being, for she knew that she had access to the Uncreated. Now she lacked nothing. Her awareness of Jesus' merciful presence, now as later, made her very contented. She was 'always cheerful and content' (DE 74).

Now she lived her entire life as an expression of God's word and of his fatherly care. She was peaceful and joyful in the depths of her being in spite of the darkness in which she experienced her faith, and even though her physical suffering increased from one day to the next. Her smile was proverbial among her sisters. They sensed that it sprang from her union with God.

But life was never really easy for Thérèse. We must remember that:

I found happiness and joy on earth uniquely in suffering, for I have suffered a great deal here below; you must let souls know about this. DE 123)

A fundamental change gradually came over her:

> If in my childhood I suffered with sadness, I no longer suffer like that
> now, but in joy and in peace. I am truly happy to suffer. (C 4 v)

Life in heaven was about to dawn; Easter, indeed, had begun in
earnest:

> I am as if resurrected – Oh, do not feel sorry for me. I have come to the
> point of being incapable of suffering, for all suffering is sweet to me.
> (DE 52)

Anguish, sorrow, offending words, the vicissitudes of health –
all these 'only touch the surface of my soul' (DE 87).

In the very depths of her being she was firmly anchored in
God. Because she was grounded in him, she felt liberated from
any adverse influence of anything apart from God, and anything
that he did not want. She revelled in images that conveyed
lightness, speed and flight through the air. She would talk of
things having 'wings'. She said that they 'flew', or were 'like a
lark' (PN 52). But everything had one chief end: the Light,
always the Light, endless Light. Now no disturbance, worry or
disillusionment could separate her from direction to the Light.
Nothing could distract her from what was essential. The reason
for this was simply that she had *faith*:

> Yes, what a grace to have faith! If I hadn't had any faith, I would have
> taken my life without a moment's hesitation. (DE 196)

Abandonment to God's will was now her only guide:

> I am not worried at all about my future, I am sure that God will do his
> will, it's the only grace I desire. (LT 221)

She lived by God's will for the present moment: 'Just for today'
(PN 5), for: 'We can put up with very much from one moment
to the next!' (DE 64):

> God gives me courage in proportion to my sufferings. I feel that, for the

time being, I could not endure any more, but I'm not afraid because, if they do increase, he will increase my courage at the same time. (DE 149)

She often repeated one of her favourite sayings (taken from her spiritual father, St John of the Cross): 'All is grace!' Gratitude was always in her heart. As ever, the only desire she had was to love more. She always wished to love more. That was the recurring theme of her prayer.

Of course she still made trivial mistakes that, strictly speaking, might be classifiable as faults, but she recognized her innate lowliness and the plentiful graces she had received. She knew that this acknowledgement was a means of drawing closer to true mercy and love:

Ever since I have been given the grace to understand also the love of the Heart of Jesus, I admit also that it has expelled all fear from my heart. The remembrance of my faults humbles me, draws me never to depend on my strength which is only weakness, but this remembrance speaks to me of mercy and love even more. When we cast our faults with entire filial confidence into the devouring fire of love, how would these not be consumed beyond return? (LT 247)

In such a perspective of boundless trust there was no room for purgatory – which she termed 'the least of my worries' (PA 1164). She possibly felt that she deserved it, yet she could not fear it. That was not possible, for she was convinced that 'the fire of love is more sanctifying than that of purgatory' (A 84 v). Moreover: 'Remembering that "charity covers a multitude of sins", I draw from this fruitful mine that Jesus has opened before me' (C 15 r).

It is interesting to compare three statements of Thérèse's at different points in her life. In 1889, she wrote while still a novice: 'Let us hurry to fashion our crown' (LT 94). Four years later, referring to her efforts to love, she conceded: 'It is not for the purpose of weaving my crown . . .' (LT 143; Letters II, 801). Lastly, in 1897, another four years on, she acknowledged: 'I haven't made my crown, but it's God who made it!' (DE 276).

En Route to Life

The time had come to meet the Lord. Thérèse's desire had reached full maturity and her reward was imminent. Now everything began to happen very rapidly, but Thérèse was expecting this:

> Never have I asked God to die young, this would have appeared to me as cowardly, but he, from my childhood, saw fit to give me the intimate conviction that my course here below would be short. (LT 258)

That is why she was in such a hurry to live intensely. As a novice, and as one who had already suffered grievously, she wrote: 'Life ... is a moment between two eternities' (LT 87).

She thought constantly of time and eternity. She saw life as a gift from God, but also as a responsibility with important consequences:

> Life is a treasure ... each moment is an eternity, an eternity of joy in heaven, an eternity of seeing God *face to face*, of being one with him! ... There is only Jesus, who *is*: all the rest *is not* ... let us love him, then, unto folly; let us save souls for him. (LT 96)

> We are greater than the whole universe, and one day we ourselves shall have a divine existence. (LT 83)

This was a vision not only of springtime but of an autumn to come, yet she was able to express her convictions more peacefully than ever before:

> At the moment of appearing before God, I understand more than ever that there is only one thing necessary, that is, to work *solely for him*. ... I would like to tell you many things that I understand now that I am at the door of eternity, but I am not dying, I am entering into Life, and all that I cannot say to you here below I will make you understand from the heights of heaven. (LT 244)

Thérèse had definitively acquired the limpid understanding of a little child. Her spiritual maturity was evident in the profound simplicity with which she saw a reflection of the divine Light in everything. As the spiritual writer Han Fortmann observed just before his own death:

> Perhaps the light is more easily accessible in the decisive hours of death than in the hustle and bustle of daily life, when death is not yet on the horizon. There are so many luminous things in life: springtime, mimosa trees, blackbirds, Mozart, love, wine, dancing, the eyes of a friend. Do they compete with the Great Clear Light? Yes, in experience that has not yet matured. The joy of things is obvious but the Great Light remains to be discovered. ... The soul has to *remind* itself that lesser lights owe their origin to the Great Light. For children, of course, this is something that is sometimes as obvious as breathing. (*Easter Rebirth*)

Was Thérèse ready to die? Yes and no. She was detached from everything, and therefore ready to receive everything:

> Since I am putting forth all my efforts to be a very little child, I have no preparations to make. Jesus himself will have to pay the expenses of the journey and the cost of entering heaven. (LT 191)

In one sense, of course, she was not ready or worthy to be united to the All-Holy. Moreover, she knew that, of herself, she would never be perfectly prepared for or deserving of that ultimate union:

> I take care to make my life an act of love, and I am no longer disturbed at being a *little* soul: on the contrary, I take delight in this. That is why I dare to hope 'my exile will be short,' but it is not because I am *prepared*: I feel that I shall never be prepared if the Lord does not see fit to transform me himself. He can do this in one instant; after all the graces he has granted me, I still await this one from his infinite mercy. (LT 224)

Thérèse had been aware for a long time that on earth she could never equal God's love for her, and this conviction rekindled her desire for heaven. There, she could love God with the fullness of his own love; without limit or distance, as she had dearly wished to do in this life. As a novice she had written: 'How I thirst for heaven, there where I shall love Jesus without reserve' (LT 79; Letters I, 514).

Now, three months before the final hour, she wrote:

> What attracts me to the homeland of heaven is the Lord's call, the hope of loving him finally as I have so much desired to love him, and the thought that I shall be able to make him loved by a multitude of souls who will bless him eternally. (LT 254; Letters I, 1142)

She was quite sure that she would continue to be an apostle on earth from her place in heaven:

> I feel that I'm about to enter into my rest. But I feel especially that my mission is about to begin, my mission of making God loved as I love him, of giving my 'little way' to souls. If God answers my desires, my heaven will be spent on earth till the end of the world. Yes, I want to spend my heaven in doing good on earth. (DE 102)

Her growing desire for heaven was now accompanied by an increasing expectation that she would die of love:

> I do not count on the illness [to go to Paradise], it is too slow a leader. I count only on *love*. Ask good Jesus that all the prayers being offered for me may serve to increase the Fire which must consume me. (LT 242)

From the outset of her religious life, Thérèse had been on fire with the words of St John of the Cross in his *Living Flame of Love*:

> It is of utmost importance that the soul should exert itself in loving so that, rapidly consuming itself, it scarcely lingers here on earth, but swiftly comes to see its God face to face.

With him she had prayed: 'Tear down the veil of this sweet encounter.'

When she later became sharply aware of the powerlessness of her love, she saw this consuming action of love as a moment when, for the last time, all her love would be concentrated in one supreme self-giving.

In her *Oblation to Merciful Love*, Thérèse had asked that this martyrdom of love would bring her to the point of death. She was to repeat this request again and again. Nevertheless, her plea had to undergo a gradual and profound transformation. At first Thérèse had expected a death more in keeping with St John of the Cross's portrayal of it: '... the wonderful transports and delicious assaults that love caused them [i.e. the saints] to experience'. But during the night of her physical and spiritual suffering, she experienced very few such 'transports' and 'assaults'. Her vision of death was to undergo a radical change. The essence of death from love would remain, but the process itself would change. Eventually, after contemplating her crucified Lord again and again, she understood that:

> Our Lord died on the Cross in agony, and yet this is the most beautiful death from love. ... To die of love is not to die in transports. (DE 73)

Finally, she arrived at the point where she said that the death from love that she wanted was 'that of Jesus on the Cross'. What this meant for her was something that she herself was to experience.

My God, I Love You

'In the evening of this life, I shall appear before you with empty hands', said Thérèse. Empty hands, yes ... but hands open to God. 'When I appear before my Beloved Spouse, I shall have only my desires to offer him' (LT 218).

The hour had come. On 30 September 1897, in the course of the afternoon, she remarked:

> It seems to me that I have never sought anything but the truth; yes, I've understood humility of heart. ... It seems to me that I am humble. (DE 205)

A little later she remarked:

> I do not regret having surrendered myself to love. Oh, no! I do not regret it, on the contrary! (DE 205)

It was now only a few minutes after seven o'clock in the evening. Why was the sun setting so soon?

Thérèse's last breath came with her last words: 'My God, I love you.' This was the supreme moment. Now she was to meet the Lord face-to-face. Now love had taken full possession of her being. This was love as deep as the ocean and more radiant than the sun. This was life and joy immeasurable: unending life with Mary and with all the saints in Heaven; eternal life with God who is all in all. Hope had finally done its work.